Someone Saw a Spider

to

Kristin –

all
good
wishes
from

Shirley Climo
1994

SOMEONE SAW A SPIDER

Spider Facts and Folktales

by Shirley Climo

ILLUSTRATED BY

Dirk Zimmer

HarperCollins*Publishers*

The quotes on pages vii and 119 from CHARLOTTE'S WEB by E.B. White © 1952 by E.B. White are reprinted by permission of Harper & Row, Publishers, Inc., and Hamish Hamilton, Ltd., London.

"The Cloud Spinner" on page 17 is adapted from "The Spider Weaver" in JAPANESE CHILDREN'S FAVORITE STORIES, edited by Florence Sakade. Used by permission of Charles E. Tuttle Co., Inc., of Tokyo, Japan.

"The Spider Brothers Make the Rainbow" on page 29 is adapted from "How the First Rainbow Was Made" from STORIES CALIFORNIA INDIANS TOLD by Anne B. Fisher, illustrated by Ruth Robbins. Parnassus Press, 1957. Used by permission of Houghton Mifflin Company.

Library of Congress Cataloging in Publication Data
Climo, Shirley.
    Someone saw a spider.

    Bibliography: p.
    Summary: A collection of myths, folklore, and
superstitions about spiders from around the world,
with some facts about how they live.
    1. Tales. 2. Spiders—Folklore. [1. Folklore.
2. Spiders—Fiction] I. Zimmer, Dirk, ill.
II. Title.
PZ8.1.C592So 1985   398.2′452944   84-45340
ISBN 0-690-04435-6
ISBN 0-690-04436-4 (lib. bdg.)

Designed by Constance Fogler
6 7 8 9 10

To David H.

"I don't know how the first spider in the early days of the world happened to think up this fancy idea of spinning a web, but she did, and it was clever of her, too. And since then, all of us spiders have had to work the same trick."

—*Charlotte of* Charlotte's Web,
by E. B. White

Contents

Someone Saw a Spider

1

Someone
Saw a Spider

SOMEONE saw a spider hanging from a thread and that was the start of a story.

For thousands of years, storytellers have been fascinated—or frightened—by spiders. Early man scratched pictures of them on the walls of his cave, and tales from ages past speak of spider magic. But spiders have been around longer than either man or magic. They were weaving their webs before mammals, before birds, even before insects appeared on earth.

Spiders live in steamy swamps and on frosted mountaintops. They scuttle over dry desert sands, burrow into dens beneath the ground, or hide within their snail-shell homes in the waters of a lake or stream. Some spiders are as small as grains of sugar; others grow big as dinner plates. Around the world we've counted 30,000 different kinds of spiders, and we think there might be three times as many more.

We still have a lot to learn about these curious creatures. Some things we do know about them are in this book, along with old stories, rhymes, and superstitions. So, the next time you see a spider, perhaps you'll understand it better.

Three thousand years ago, the Greeks told a tale about the first spider. That myth is called "Arachne's Gift."

Arachne's Gift

AGES ago, on the shores of the Aegean Sea, there lived a Greek maiden named Arachne. She was special, for Arachne had a gift.

As a baby, she lay content in her cradle, trying to braid the sunbeams that danced above her head.

As a small child, while her friends struggled to tie the thongs on their sandals, Arachne strung daisies into chains and made baskets, tiny as hummingbird nests, from weeds and grasses.

And, as soon as she grew tall enough to stand upon a stool and touch the top of a loom, Arachne began to weave.

At first, she snarled the strands of wool and tangled her shuttle in the web of strings. But even though her hands ached and her eyes smarted, she would rip out her mistakes and begin again. Her friends thought Arachne strange, always shut away, always spinning and weaving.

"Arachne! Arachne!" they would tease her through the window. "You'll not catch us in your net!"

Then Arachne would close the heavy wooden shutters, but the thump, thump of her treadle and the swish, swish of her reed could still be heard, far into the night.

Finally the day came when she no longer made mistakes. The wool Arachne spun was as warm as summer and light as a thistle puff. The cloth she wove was so delicate that a moth would leave behind its footprint, yet so strong no spear could pierce it. The same voices that had taunted Arachne now pleaded to buy a robe or wrap of her making.

"There's not gold enough in Greece to repay me for your teasing," she told them.

Now she kept the shutters wide open for all to admire her skill.

The fame of Arachne the Spinner spread across the countryside, and even the nymphs slipped out from their secret hideaways to watch her at her work.

"Ah, Arachne!" cried one. "Your shuttle flies fast as an arrow from Diana's bow!"

Arachne smiled. "Even swifter."

"You have a gift from the gods," said another.

Arachne scowled. "I have only myself to thank for my talents."

"But surely the goddess Minerva was your teacher?" asked a third.

"Minerva!" Arachne turned angrily to the nymphs. "Why, should I meet that noble hag, it's I who could teach her a trick or two!"

The nymphs gasped and disappeared like wisps of fog among the trees. But they whispered Arachne's terrible boast to others. Now people spoke not of her clever fingers but of her bold tongue.

"Take care, Arachne," they warned. "Nothing said or done escapes the gods on Mount Olympus."

Their advice was as annoying to Arachne as the buzzing of mosquitoes. "Should the gods be watching, it is because they envy me!"

Arachne went on with her weaving. As she pushed the shuttle back and forth, it seemed to sing, "None can match Arachne, None can match Arachne."

One midnight, something scratched softly on her shutters. A branch, thought Arachne, blown by the wind, but she opened her door and peered out. All she saw was the silhouette of an owl, perched on a limb of an olive tree, black against the moon. Then a bent old woman, wrapped in a shawl, stepped from the shadows.

"Come in and rest," Arachne offered.

"I seek not shelter but only to look upon your weaving."

"Then you come too late," Arachne replied. "My work's best seen by light of dawn."

The old crone pushed past Arachne to the loom. Her eyes darted up and down the tapestry.

"You weave splendidly," she said, rubbing her bony fingers over the cloth.

"Yes," agreed Arachne. "For I am different from most, and better than any."

"Except Minerva," the stranger said sharply. "Mind, even you cannot compete with that goddess."

"I wish I had the chance!" Arachne stretched out her hands. "I am young and my fingers are nimble. Minerva is old, like you, Grandmother. Her glory is past."

"Ask forgiveness, child, for such foolish words." The woman's voice was muffled by her cloak.

Arachne shrugged. "My weaving speaks for me."

"Then your wish shall be granted." The squinted eyes opened wide and the hands upon Arachne's loom spread out strong, without a wrinkle. "Here, on the morrow, you shall have the contest you desire."

"With whom?" asked Arachne.

There was a sudden rush of cold wind, and the oil lamp sputtered. Arachne shivered and rubbed her eyes. Her visitor had vanished. Through the door, yet ajar, Arachne saw the owl flap silently up from the olive tree. It was said that whenever Minerva journeyed into the mortal world, her owl always went with her.

"With Minerva," whispered Arachne to the empty room. "The goddess herself has challenged me."

Arachne could not sleep that night. To steady her mind and her hands, she carded and spun and sorted her wools, choosing only the softest and finest. Then she strung her loom with a web of new, strong threads. She had just tightened the last peg when her door burst open.

Minerva stood on the doorstep, bright as the rising sun. The goddess wore a shining breastplate, and a golden helmet crowned her head. The owl sat on her shoulder, its talons curled about a jeweled guard. But the loom Minerva brought was made of wood and no grander than Arachne's own. Minerva stared at Arachne, her gray eyes glinting with sparks, like those struck from a flint.

Arachne met her gaze. Even now she would not apologize.

Without a word, the contest began. The nymphs grew dizzy watching, so fast did the fingers of the weavers skim across their looms.

The goddess wove with the colors of the heavens. She used the golden rays of the sun and the blue from the midday sky. She drew palest pinks and greens and lavenders from the rainbow and worked with silver spun from starshine.

The story Minerva spun was of the heavens, too, scenes of the dozen most powerful gods. Father Jupiter sat upon his throne, and Neptune, ruler of the sea, rose up from bubbling waters. Apollo scattered the clouds with his chariot, and Diana arched her arrow at the moon. Minerva placed herself, victorious, in the center of her cloth. In the corners she embroidered smaller figures. These were the unhappy humans who dared to defy the gods.

"Arachne!" the nymphs said softly. "See how Minerva warns you!"

Arachne ignored them. Nor did she listen to the song of her shuttle as it sighed, "Do not mock Minerva, Do not mock Minerva."

Arachne worked with the colors of the earth. Her oranges and scarlets were the shades of spring poppies.

She picked yellow from the summer daisies and purple from autumn grapes. Her gray was soft as winter's mist, but her blue was bright, as if she'd dipped her yarn into the sea.

Arachne, too, put the gods into her patterns. But the tales she chose to tell were dreadful.

She pictured Minerva, defeated in battle, with her owl a cowering sparrow. She showed the goddess Juno in a jealous rage. She dressed Jupiter as a swan, foolish in his feathers, and again disguised as a bull. So artful was her hand that the swan seemed about to trumpet and the bull to bellow aloud.

At nightfall, Minerva stepped back from her loom. "The contest is over. My work is finished."

The nymphs crowded about Minerva's glowing tapestry. "Ah!" they cried, shading their eyes, for it was like looking at the sun itself. Then they peeked over their shoulders at Arachne's handiwork. The nymphs were speechless.

"Who is the winner?" Minerva demanded.

"Judge for yourself," answered Arachne.

Minerva wheeled about and stared in disbelief at Arachne's loom. An insult to the gods was stitched in every splendid scene. "Wretch!" she shrieked.

Arachne held her head high and smiled. "My work deserves praise, for it is as perfect as your own."

Snatching Arachne's shuttle, Minerva tore down the weaving. "This is what your wickedness deserves!" she declared.

Arachne looked down at her tapestry, in shreds on the floor. Nothing was left of her marvelous work but a single strand, dangling from the frame. With shaking fingers, Arachne seized it and tied it tight around her neck.

"Hold!" Minerva's hand loosened the knot. "You wish to hang, and so you shall, but in another manner."

Minerva drew a flask from the folds of her tunic. When she unstoppered it, fumes rose like smoke, for within were the juices of a powerful plant called aconite. "This is my gift to you," said the goddess, sprinkling a few drops on Arachne's head.

Arachne's skin tingled, then grew numb. She felt weightless as a cloud. It seemed as if this were the way she was born to be.

"Since you are proud to be different, you shall be like no other on earth," spoke Minerva.

The nymphs saw Arachne change before their very eyes. Her body shrank smaller and smaller. Eight slender legs replaced her fingers. Her nose and her ears disappeared; her hair fell away. But her mouth remained, and the last thing that the nymphs saw of Arachne was her proud smile. Now some strange new creature hung suspended from the loom.

"Live," said Minerva, "and spin your wondrous webs forevermore." So saying, the goddess left.

The thunderstruck nymphs were silent. As they watched, the creature slowly spun its way to the top of the frame and began to weave a web. Arachne the maiden had been transformed into the first of the world's spiders. And, for Arachne the spider, work had just begun.

Arachne's Gifts

ARACHNE gave her name, which means "spider" in Greek, to all her kin. Although only spiders can spin, scorpions, mites, and ticks are close cousins and are *arachnids*, too.

The Greek myth about Arachne was borrowed by the Romans. These ancient Romans "read" spiderwebs, believing that by watching a spider move within its web they might foresee the future. Soon the idea began to grow that spiders were not only fortune-tellers but fortune bringers as well. Even today, many think that a spider in the home brings luck to all who live there.

In Britain, most people welcome the money spider

as a house guest. This small spider brings wealth, especially if the finder tosses it—very gently—over his left shoulder. In Polynesia, it is said that if a spider drops down in front of you, it is a sure sign you will get a present.

Here are some of Arachne's other gifts:

A spider at night brings joy and delight;
A spider seen in the morning brings you a warning.
(Europe and U.S.A.)

If a spider creeps across you, it is measuring you for new clothes. If it crawls into your pocket, you will always have money. *(Europe and U.S.A.)*

Spider in the corner, money in the chest. *(U.S.A.)*

Should a spider weave its web across the door, company is coming. *(U.S.A.)*

Don't sweep down the cobwebs from the rafters, for if a spider falls from the ceiling, you'll receive unexpected riches. *(U.S.A.)*

A spider hanging over your head means you will get a letter. *(U.S.A.)*

If you walk into a spiderweb, you will meet a friend that day. *(U.S.A.)*

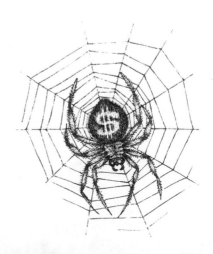

2

Cobwebs
in the Sky

HAVE you ever seen a spider sailing through the sky? In the fall, or in the spring, you may see some spider astronauts. Less than a century ago, people believed that spiders could fly and that they used their legs as wings. But those spiders overhead aren't flying. They're floating.

When baby spiders hatch, they spin draglines and then cling to them like trapeze artists and glide through the air. Sometimes the breeze blows them only a few feet; other times they will travel for hundreds of miles. Bits of their thread have even been found wrapped around the funnels of ships far out at sea. By ballooning, spiders find new homes and spread their kind the world around. But we've only understood this recently.

Two thousand years ago, when a Roman named Pliny saw webs above his head, he declared, "It's raining wool!"

Over the years, others thought the webs were shreds of goosedown drifting through the air. That's why we call spider silk "gossamer," which comes from "goose summer."

In old Japan, some saw these cobwebs in the sky and gave another explanation. They told the story of "The Cloud Spinner."

The Cloud Spinner

YOSAKU marched up and down the neat rows of radishes and cabbages and beans. He was proud as a warrior inspecting his soldiers. This year his garden grew especially well.

"Just so! Just so!" The farmer matched his words to the slap-slap of his feet in their wooden *geta*.

On occasion, Yosaku planted his sandals firmly, swung his hoe like a samurai sword, and shouted, "Off with your head!" A weed would topple.

When he came to the last row of cabbages, Yosaku stopped and wiped his face on the sleeve of his *kimono*. Although low in the sky, the sun was hot, and there was no shadow but his own. Yet he was not alone. Between two cabbage stalks stretched a spiderweb, and in the center sat a handsome spider. Its body, dark as polished teak, was striped with gray that shone like silver in the sunlight.

"Greetings," said Yosaku politely. "You honor me by visiting my garden." He stepped back, so as not to disturb his guest. His heel struck something much too soft for a cabbage, far too thick for a bean.

"Sssssss!" A huge and ugly snake slipped over his sandal.

"Ara!" exclaimed Yosaku, waving his hoe.

The snake's tongue darted in and out of its mouth, its bright, cold eye fixed upon the spider. The spider froze, as if tied in its own ropes.

"Off with your head!" Yosaku shouted at the snake.

But as he brought down the hoe, the handle caught and ripped the full sleeve of his *kimono*. Yosaku missed, and the snake slithered away. The spider ran down from its web and disappeared among the cabbages.

Yosaku looked at his torn sleeve. The *kimono* was beyond mending and he had no other, for Yosaku was poor. "Just so!" he said, but sadly now, and went home to his bowl of rice and bed-mat.

That night Yosaku slept soundly until the Hour of the Ox, when a tiny voice, calling from the courtyard, awakened him.

"Mr. Yosaku!"

"Eh?" mumbled Yosaku. Perhaps his ears were playing tricks.

"Honorable Mr. Yosaku!"

Yosaku tied his old *kimono* tight and padded to the door. There stood a young girl. Her robe was of rich black silk stitched with rows of silver thread. Yosaku blinked. Perhaps his eyes tricked him, too.

The girl bowed low. "You are in need of new *kimono?*"

Yosaku stared down on the girl's dark glossy head. She reminded him of something, but he was too sleepy to remember what. "So I am," he answered.

She looked up at him and smiled shyly. "If you will allow, I would be pleased to weave new cloth for *kimono.*"

Yosaku, astounded by such a grand offering, slid the door wide. "You are welcome in my house."

He offered tea to the girl, but she refused and went directly to the weaving room. When Yosaku lit the lantern overhead, he was ashamed by the cobwebs on the ceiling and the dust layered on the loom. But the girl seemed not to notice and set at once to sorting his small store of cotton. Yosaku went back to sleep on his mat again, and soon was snoring to the rhythm of the loom. When he awoke in the morning, there were seven new *kimono*, neatly laid out next to his mat.

Yosaku rubbed his eyes. "How can this be?" He ran to the weaving room. "Already you made new *kimono* for every day of the week!"

"Do not question, Honorable Yosaku." The girl looked modestly down at her hands. "And please do not come into this room while I work."

Yosaku bobbed his head. "It shall be as you wish," he agreed. "I shall not trouble you."

It was Yosaku himself who was troubled. Although he placed bean-jam buns and tea on a lacquered tray outside the closed door of the weaving room, nothing was touched. In the evening he brought tempting rice cakes, but in the morning the plate was still piled high. Yet each day the girl presented him with new lengths of cloth, finer than any he'd ever seen.

To his thanks, she replied, "It is I who am grateful."

Yosaku asked nothing, not even the girl's name, but his curiosity was growing even greater than the stack of *kimono* in his cupboard. So, at the week's end, he slipped out of his sandals and tiptoed to the window of the weaving room. Slowly, softly he slid back the rice-paper screen. In the center of the room sat his visitor at the newly strung loom. Only it was not the young girl. It was a giant spider!

"Aaaah!" Yosaku clapped his hand over his mouth.

All his life he had heard tales of goblin-spiders. But goblins were nighttime demons, and this was mid-day. He peeped again at the strange spider-girl. She was eating, and what she was eating was even stranger. She was swallowing great mouthfuls of cotton and spinning it out as finished thread.

No wonder the girl was not hungry!

Yosaku watched as all eight of the spider's legs, working together, wove the thread into cloth.

No wonder the girl had done so much so quickly!

The black and gray pattern of the spider's back was the same as that on the girl's robe. Although much bigger, this was the same spider he'd rescued from the snake. Yosaku was sure of it.

Yosaku crept away from the window. He had come close to spoiling the spider-girl's secret. But he had an idea of his own. His store of cotton was small and his garden was large. He'd harvest some vegetables and sell them in the market at Kyoto. There he would buy such a big bundle of cotton that the spider-girl would never go hungry.

At sunrise, Yosaku piled his cart high with fresh radishes and cabbages and beans and pulled it up and over the hill to Kyoto. At sunset, he returned with the cart spilling over with cotton. Although the load of cotton was much lighter than the load of vegetables, his arms ached from all the pulling and pushing. When he neared his own fields again, he sat down to rest. Yosaku's eyelids drooped. His mouth dropped open and his chin sagged on his chest. Dozing, he did not see the snake that wriggled toward his cart.

The snake saw Yosaku. This farmer had cheated it of a delicious spider supper! The snake was angry still. Hissing softly, the snake crawled up and over the sides of the cart and into the bundle of cotton. Yosaku yawned and stretched, never realizing what had awakened him, never noticing that his load was a trifle heavier as he trudged on home.

That night Yosaku did not put the rice cakes outside the weaving room door. He left the huge mountain of cotton instead. In the morning, every shred was gone.

As soon as he heard the thud of the treadle, Yosaku padded to the weaving room window and slid aside the panel. As before, the girl sat at the loom in the form of the spider, gobbling up the cotton as if it were sugary

candy. Only a few handfuls of fluff remained. Then, as if he were watching a puppet play, Yosaku saw:

. . . the snake spring from the last bit of cotton and rattle its tail

. . . the spider shriek, in her young girl's voice

. . . the snake unhinge its jaws to swallow the spider

. . . the spider frantically wave her legs

. . . the snake snap—and miss!

The spider gave a jump and hopped through the window, right over Yosaku's head. The snake followed, slithering over his shoulder. Yosaku stared open mouthed after both of them. When he had gathered his wits together, he ran into the house for his hoe.

The spider scrambled across the courtyard with the hungry snake in pursuit. She was too stuffed with cotton to move at full speed, and second by second the space between them closed.

The sun was high overhead, and sunbeams were falling straight as bamboo poles into the courtyard. In her haste, the spider stumbled, and then discovered that a sun ray stuck to a bit of thread in her mouth. The spider dangled for a moment and then, spinning out more thread as she went, she climbed straight up the sunbeam to the safety of the sky.

By the time Yosaku reached the courtyard he could not see the spider-girl anywhere. But, in a corner of the courtyard, he spied the snake, tying itself in knots with anger. Yosaku swung his hoe.

"Off with your head!"

This time he chopped the serpent in two, and both halves wiggled away in different directions.

"Just so."

Yosaku brushed off his new kimono and looked up. He saw a small cloud, like a tuft of white cotton, float through the air. Although he could not imagine how she got there, Yosaku knew where the spider-girl was. She was spinning her cotton, high overhead, and showing her thanks in her own special way.

"Kumo!" shouted Yosaku, and the breeze carried his salute to the spider in the sky.

That's why, in Japan, when fleecy clouds dot the sky, people say it must be the work of the spider-girl. Even today, a spider and a cloud share the same name: *Kumo.*

There was an old woman tossed in a basket
   Seventeen times as high as the moon;
But where she was going no mortal could tell,
   For under her arm she carried a broom.

"Old Woman, Old Woman, Old Woman," said I,
   "Whither, oh whither, oh whither so high?"
"To sweep the cobwebs out of the sky,
   But I'll be with you by and by."

—Nursery rhyme

3

Spiders, Sun, and Showers

TO American Indians, spiders were magic creatures that belonged to the sky as well as to the earth. Because the spokes of spiderwebs stretch out like sunbeams, the Indians associated spiders with the sun itself. Many believed that when warriors died they climbed up to the heavens on ropes of spider silk.

The Apache people honored Grandfather Spider, for it was he who made a ladder of sunbeams so they might climb up from the center of the earth.

The Hopis had Gogyeng Sowuhti, which means Grandmother Spider. She was the messenger of the Sun Spirit, and she helped the Hopis on their journey from the darkness below to sunshine above.

The Cherokees also loved Grandmother Spider. In their stories, she brought the first fire into the world by snatching a bit of the sun.

The Chippewas hung real spiderwebs on the hoops

of their babies' cradleboards so that any harm floating in the air would be caught in the web.

Tolowa Indians of northern California told how a clever spider stole some of the moon. Their neighbors, the Achomawi, assigned a different, but equally difficult, heavenly task to spiders. "The Spider Brothers Make the Rainbow" is an Achomawi myth.

The Spider Brothers
Make the Rainbow

IT STORMED, it showered, it drizzled, and it dripped.
Then it stormed again.

The Indians did not know how many moons it had
been raining, for the moon, as well as the sun, was
hidden behind the clouds. The rain rinsed the snowcap
from Mount Shasta. Streams swelled over their banks,
and the smallest trickles spilled like waterfalls.

The Achomawi men could not go hunting or seed-
gathering. Water dripped down the smoke holes of the
houses and put out the cooking fires of the Achomawi

women. So the chief of that tribe put on his feather headdress and shook his deer-toe rattle and did a no-more-rain dance. Still the clouds came.

"Coyote has been on earth longer than anyone else," said the chief. "He will know what to do."

The chief found Coyote in his cave. Coyote was miserable, too, for his fur was so wet that all the fleas had jumped behind his ears to stay dry.

"I will ask Old-Man-Above to send back the sun," said Coyote. He cleared his throat and threw back his head. "Yeow-oow-oooooh!"

Coyote howled so loudly that rocks rolled down the mountainside and pine cones shook loose from the trees. But Old-Man-Above was making so much thunder that he did not hear.

Coyote sat down and scratched and thought about ways to catch the attention of Old-Man-Above.

"Climb to the top of Mount Shasta," the coyote finally said to the chief. "Take all of your people, and I will meet you there."

The Indians trudged one way up the mountain trail while Coyote ran another way through the woods. There he found Spider Woman swinging high in a cedar tree.

"Will you help to bring back the sun?" asked Coyote in his softest, sweetest voice.

"I'm too old and too tired to be of use," said Spider Woman, "but my sixty sons live on the branch above. Perhaps one of them will help you."

Spider Woman's two youngest sons had had quite enough of hanging about in a wet web.

"We'll do what we can," cried one Spider Brother.

"Whatever it is," cried the other.

"Follow me," said Coyote, and turned toward the mountain trail.

Just beyond the big gray rock and over the fallen tree, they met the Two White-footed Mouse Boys, searching for acorns among the soggy leaves.

"We're going up Mount Shasta to chase away the clouds," Coyote said. "Will you help us?"

The snowy white feet of the mice were all caked with mud.

"We'll do what we can," they promised.

Now there were five marching up the mountain-side. As they passed a hollow stump, Weasel Man poked out his pointy nose. The dampness made Weasel Man ache all over, so when the coyote explained the reason for their journey, the weasel answered:

"Then I'll come along and do whatever I can."

The Two White-footed Mouse Boys shivered. What Weasel Man could do was to have them for dinner. But the weasel was soaked to the skin and too miserable to misbehave.

By and by the six saw Red Fox Woman pawing about in a berry bush.

"We're on our way to ask Old-Man-Above to send back the sun," called Coyote.

"I will go, too," she said.

Out from under the bush jumped Rabbit Woman. She'd been hiding from hungry Red Fox Woman. But her burrow was awash with water, and if the Spider Brothers and the Mouse Boys and Weasel Man and Red Fox Woman were all going to help Coyote to stop the rain, then . . .

"So shall I," said Rabbit Woman.

Coyote led the parade to the top of Mount Shasta, which is a very high mountain indeed. There the Indians were waiting for him. Red Fox Woman looked at their bows and arrows and shuddered. The white-footed mice looked at the weasel and trembled. Rabbit Woman looked at Red Fox Woman and twitched. The Spider Brothers sat down and rubbed their sixteen legs, which smarted after such a long, steep climb. Everyone wondered what Coyote had in mind.

"Old-Man-Above did not notice the dancing of the chief, nor did he listen to my song," admitted Coyote. "Someone must go up to the sky and whisper in his ear."

"Who?" asked Weasel Man.

"The Spider Brothers," said Coyote.

The Spider Brothers! Indians and animals shook their heads. The spiders were the smallest and weakest among them.

"And after Old-Man-Above promises to send back the sun, they'll swing back to earth on their spinning ropes."

"We can swing down on our ropes, as you say, Coyote . . ." said one of the Spider Brothers.

"But how shall we get up?" finished the other brother.

"We'll *blow* you up!" cried Coyote.

The spiders stared at each other. The rest of the animals looked at Coyote as if his brains had grown moss.

Coyote turned to the chief. "Call your best bowmen."

Two Indians stepped forward and put arrows to their bows.

"Pull hard and aim well," Coyote warned, "for each must strike the same spot in the sky."

The two braves stretched their bowstrings back, and with a loud twang their arrows leapt away. They traveled side by side, straight up, until both pierced a hole in the gray clouds and those below could see blue sky.

"Now, blow!" cried Coyote, puffing out his cheeks.

The animals and the Indians were so weary from their climb that they'd scarcely any breath left at all.

"Aiyeee!" the Indians wheezed.

"Phoooo!" sputtered the Mouse Boys.

"Whiffff!" sighed Red Fox Woman and Rabbit Woman.

Weasel Man couldn't get out a gasp. The Spider Brothers drifted a few feet in the air and then thudded to the ground.

"My plan will never work unless we work together," scolded Coyote. "Try again, with all your might, and all at once. One!"

Everyone stood straight.

"Two!"

Everyone took a deep breath.

The spiders gave a spring.

"Three!"

Everyone blew.

Up and up soared the Spider Brothers. They sailed into the sky, spinning their ropes behind them. Those on the ground kept huffing and puffing until they all were as red in the face as Red Fox Woman. They blew until none had so much as a hiccup left.

The spiders were almost to the arrow hole. One

of them reached up with three of his legs and caught the edge of a cloud. The second brother grabbed the remaining five legs of the first. The spiders bobbed about in midair.

"Ooooh!" moaned Coyote and his companions.

Their sighs made just enough breeze to blow the brothers through the hole, and the two spiders disappeared from sight.

Those below hunkered down on their legs or their tails and rested. Up above, the weary spiders collapsed on the cloud and fell asleep.

"What are you two specks doing up here?" a voice roared.

The spiders' sixteen eyes flew open. Old-Man-Above himself was striding toward them, hurling lightning bolts and stamping thunder with every footstep.

"We're not specks. We're spiders," said one brother in a shaky voice.

"We've come with a message from earth," whispered the other.

Old-Man-Above cupped a hand behind his ear. "Eh?"

The brothers stood on tiptoe. "We ask you—please—to send back the sun."

"But how did you get up here?" Old-Man-Above pulled on his white whiskers and looked puzzled.

The Spider Brothers took turns in telling how Coyote had scratched out a plan and how everyone had helped to send them up.

Old-Man-Above beamed as bright as the sun, which lay forgotten at his feet. "All my earth people working together! Man and coyote! Mouse and weasel! Fox and rabbit! And you two specks as well."

"Spiders," corrected the first brother.

Old-Man-Above peered through the hole in the sky. "It does look a little damp down there. Perhaps I should put away the clouds for a while."

"Thank you," said both spiders together.

"But I can't have you creatures climbing up here and bothering me every time you want a change in weather." Old-Man-Above scowled, black as a thunderhead. The spiders squirmed.

"Perhaps," suggested one of them timidly, "you could make a rain-clear sign so that we will know when the sun is returning."

Old-Man-Above scratched behind his ear. "I know," he shouted, "a *fox tail*!"

His roar split the clouds, and the spiders had to hold tight to one another to keep from slipping off altogether. They looked about, but there was nothing like a fox tail anywhere.

"Think!" Old-Man-Above waggled his finger at them. "Imagine a big, bright, beautiful fox tail!"

The first brother's mind was as empty as a basket with a hole in it. Then he remembered Red Fox Woman's bushy tail, and, as he did, a streak of red appeared across the sky.

The second brother thought about Coyote's fuzzy tail instead, and a band of that same yellow brushed up against the red. Then one thought wistfully of the green forests below, and the other thought of the blue sky soon to come. Together the spiders dreamed about the soft purple shadows of twilight and of safe, snug evenings in their own web.

"Wonderful!" exclaimed Old-Man-Above. "Just look what thinking can do!"

As if a giant fox tail had been dipped into a paint pot, red, yellow, green, blue, and violet arched across the sky.

"That is my rain-clear sign," Old-Man-Above said, pleased. "Whenever the rain is over, I'll push aside the clouds and hang this striped fox tail for all to see." He nodded to the awestruck spiders. "Now take that message down to your friends below."

The Spider Brothers were only too glad to obey. They tied their ropes tightly to the edge of the hole and began to scramble down.

"Mind!" shouted Old-Man-Above after them. "Tell those Indians not to shoot any more holes in my sky!" And as soon as the Spider Brothers had safely touched ground, he plugged up the hole with a cloud.

All this had taken quite a bit of time, so when the spiders stepped down on Mount Shasta, they found everything in a turmoil. Spider Woman was wailing that she'd lost her two favorite sons. The Indians were quarreling among themselves. Weasel Man was nipping at the Mouse Boys, and once again Rabbit Woman was hiding from Red Fox Woman. Coyote had buried his nose in his paws, for everyone blamed him. The Spider Brothers almost wished they'd stayed above.

"Old-Man-Above listened to us," began one proudly.

"He has sent a rain-clear sign," interrupted the other.

But with all the whining and the howling, snarling and snapping, none paid heed to the spiders. So they shouted in chorus, and so strongly that they used up their voices forever:

"The rain is over! See the sky!"

Spider Woman stopped crying and the Indians stopped fighting. Coyote looked up. The Two White-footed Mouse Boys and Weasel Man and Red Fox Woman and Rabbit Woman closed their mouths and lifted their eyes. Above their heads the world's first rainbow stretched across the sky.

"Ahhhhhh!" cried the animals and the Indians.

They cheered so long and loud the Spider Brothers thought they might be blown aloft again. But they held tight to their ropes, anchored themselves to a tree, and began to make more rain-clear signs, spun right within their own webs.

From that time on, Old-Man-Above has always hung a bright-striped fox tail in the sky to signal the return of the sun. And, to this day, smaller rainbows sparkle within wet spiderwebs, just as the Spider Brothers first made them.

Spider
the Weatherman

Eeensie beensie spider climbed up the water spout.
Down came the rain and washed the spider out.
Out came the sun and dried up all the rain, and
Eeensie beensie spider crawled up the spout again.
—American finger-play song

YOU have probably sung that song. But maybe you
didn't know that spiders really are weather-watchers.
They spin their webs outside when the weather is fine,
but seek snug shelter when it is foul. That is why sun
or storms often play an important part in spider stories.

In America, they still repeat these old-time spider forecasts:

When spiders spin their webs 'fore noon,
Sunny weather's coming soon.

If spiders abandon their webs, a storm is on the way.

Spider webs floating at autumn sunset,
Night frost to follow, on this you can bet.

If spiderwebs in the air do fly, the spell will soon be very dry.

If you step on a spider, you'll bring on rain.

The more spiders that creep indoors in the fall, the colder the winter to come.

The Chicchansee Indians of California said: "When tarantulas walk uphill, the skies will weep."

But, beware! Should a spiderweb fall down without any reason, a Hebrew superstition holds that a flood will follow.

4

Spider the
Story Spinner

The wisdom of Ananse is greater than that
of all the world put together.
　　　　　　　　　　—*Gold Coast proverb*

QUICK little spiders appear to be quite clever, so many
African peoples thought they must be just as bright as
they were busy.

Spiders really aren't so smart. They rely on their
instinct. How a spider will act and react for its entire
lifetime is programmed, like a computer, before it even
hatches.

According to legend, Ananse, the spider hero of
West Africa, once collected all the knowledge in the
world. He became the owner of every story told, and
so, of course, many of the tales are about him. Ananse
is most often a chief in stories that the Ashanti tell. But

in this tale from Liberia, he is a trickster called simply Oldman Spider.

"How Spider Got His Waistline" explains why a spider looks and behaves the way it does. Oldman Spider does what no real arachnid could ever do. He learns a lesson.

How Spider
Got His Waistline

LONG ago, in Liberia, the spider was far bigger and rounder than he is now, for he was always hungry and always stuffing his stomach. His skin stretched over his belly tight as the skin on a drum, and his eight legs poked out at the sides, like drumsticks. He strutted about boldly in broad daylight, on the lookout for anything tasty.

Each year, in that part of Africa, there came a season when the clouds held back the rains. Rivers grew shallow, scarcely deep enough to rinse the back of the smallest hippo. Ponds shrank to puddles, and the noses of the crocodiles pushed up through the mud. Antelopes browsed higher on the plains and birds flew farther from their nests in search of food.

Oldman Spider, too, was hungrier than ever. His stomach rumbled, and his wife and children grumbled.

"Leopard has food to spare," said Spider's wife. "His fish basket is always full."

"Leopard's not likely to help *me*," replied Spider, remembering the time he had stung Leopard's nose.

"Then help yourself," said the wife.

"And get squashed by a great, toe-nailed paw?" squealed Spider. "No, thank you!"

"Your twenty-four children are crying," his wife complained. "There's not even a fly to share among them."

Spider looked up at the roof-pole of his hut, which was where he hung his stores. No silk-wrapped morsels swung in the net. His wife was right. But, then, Spider usually agreed with her, for she was bigger than he was.

"Leave things to me," said Spider. "My stomach's empty, but my head's still full of wits."

Oldman Spider hurried out the doorhole of his hut, just as the last light of the sun was turning the sky to rusty red. He scrambled along the path that led from his home to the river's edge, and there Spider spotted Leopard himself. His mouth watered as he watched Leopard shake bait into a woven basket and place the basket trap on the muddy river bottom. Spider could almost smell the fine, fresh fish that would soon be flopping in that trap. But Oldman Spider was too wise to be hasty.

"If I snatch Leopard's catch, then Leopard will surely snatch me," said he to himself. "First I must have a plan." So, when Leopard stalked uphill to his den, Spider sat down to think.

Something else moved by the river's edge.

Firefly perched on the top of a reed, weakly fluttering his wings. Only a pale flicker of light glowed from beneath them.

"Good evening, friend Firefly," called Spider.

Firefly started, and looked about. "Oh! It's *you*, Spider. You're no friend to me." Firefly's voice was almost as faint as his light.

"A shame," said Spider, "to find you so weak from hunger. But then," he added, "I'm hungry, too."

"You'll not eat me!" shrieked Firefly.

"Such an idea!" Spider answered, in a honey-sweet tone. "In times like these, we smaller creatures must stick together."

"It's a bad end for any *you* stick to," said Firefly.

"You don't understand," whispered Oldman Spider. "I mean we should work together. You use your light—and I'll use my head."

"How so?" asked Firefly, twitching nervously as Spider inched closer.

"Upstream is Leopard's fish trap." Spider waved a couple of legs in that direction. "What a greedy fellow!" Spider shuddered. "I dare not borrow even the smallest of his fish in daylight. He's sure to see me. Nor can I take one by night, for I can't see it. But if you, dear firefly, were to hover high above the basket, I might empty the trap with ease by your light."

"I am not a thief," said Firefly firmly.

"Of course not!" Spider sounded shocked. "You shan't steal a thing yourself. But if your light helps me, what's the harm in that?"

"What's the good, either?" asked Firefly.

"We're partners. Partners share. And you'll get your share of the fish as well."

"It's slippery work," began Firefly doubtfully.

"Don't be selfish," Spider interrupted.

Firefly blinked. He was not nearly so clever as spider, but he was kind of heart. "If you put it that way . . ."

"Agreed!" Spider chuckled softly. He knew he had trapped Firefly in a web of words.

When the sun had fully set, and the sky turned dark above the mahogany trees, Spider and Firefly went to the river's edge beneath Leopard's den. All was quiet, save for the sound of Leopard's snoring. Firefly darted back and forth above the basket trap, his light reflecting in the still, shallow water below. By that light, Spider spun a stout rope and tied it to the basket's handle. Then, heaving and hauling with all his might, Spider pulled Leopard's basket up onto the bank. In it were four fat fish.

If Leopard heard a swish or splash, he thought it nothing more than a clumsy crocodile. When he saw the twinkle of firefly's light, he supposed it was a shooting star. And he went back to sleep.

With Firefly's help, Spider strung the fish together, and the two dragged the bundle down the path to Spider's home.

When the twenty-four spiderlings saw the fish, they

began fighting and biting amongst themselves, and the quarreling was worse than their crying had been.

"Quiet!" ordered Oldman Spider, and divided each of the four fish into six pieces. Soon the little spiders' mouths were too full to make any noise at all.

"Where is my share?" asked Firefly.

"Why, six times four is twenty-four, with none left over," explained Spider.

Firefly was no better with numbers than he was with words, so he said nothing.

"Tomorrow night," promised Spider.

The following night was just as the first, except that this time Spider pulled five fish from Leopard's basket. After he and Firefly had gotten them to his hut, Spider divided four of the fish among the twenty-four spiderlings and served up the fifth to himself and his wife.

"Where is my piece?" asked Firefly.

"It was I who took the risk as well as the fish," mumbled Spider between bites. "Perhaps tomorrow night."

Firefly had no answer for that.

On the third night, Firefly once again shone his light while Spider raised the basket. Six fish wiggled within. Spider gave four fish to his children and split one between his wife and himself. Then he spun a silken thread around the last fish and tossed it into the net that hung from the roof beam.

"That should be mine!" cried Firefly.

Spider clucked his tongue. "I must save for a rainy day. And you must have patience, friend. Doesn't tomorrow always come?"

Firefly had to admit that was true.

The next evening was blacker than the inside of an anthill at midnight. The moon hid her face behind the clouds and not a single star sparkled in the sky. The only light came from Firefly, circling slowly above the river. Spider worked quickly by that glow. The basket was not as heavy as before, and when Spider upended it upon the bank, just one fish flopped out.

"Leopard's cheating me!" complained Spider.

Firefly did not reply. Although his brain was not so bright as his light, Firefly began to wonder who was cheating whom. If he did not get his fair share of four or five or six fish, it was certain he was not going to get so much as a sniff of just one. Something besides hunger was gnawing at Firefly. He felt dishonest.

Without a word, Firefly put out his light.

"Brother Firefly!" shouted Spider. "Brighten up!"

But Firefly had flown away, and Spider was left alone in the darkness.

Spider couldn't see a leg before his face. Still, he could feel, so he twisted a strong thread about the tail of the scaly, slippery fish and started home, dragging the fish behind him.

The path was tangled with prickly vines, and sharp stones stung Spider's feet. That was because Spider wasn't on the path at all.

The fish he pulled grew heavier with every step. That was because Spider wasn't going downhill to his own hut, but stumbling uphill, straight toward Leopard's den.

"Tricky Firefly!" muttered Spider. "Not to be

trusted." And he stopped to rest and have just a bit of fish to build up his strength.

Spider stopped more and more often, and each time he had another bite. As Oldman Spider got fuller, the fish got lighter. Soon nothing was left of the fish but the backbone and tail.

"I'll tell my wife that Firefly ate it," said Spider.

At last Spider made out the shadow of a doorhole before him. Thinking he was home, he tiptoed right inside. All was quiet. Leopard was dozing and dreaming, without a sigh or snore.

"For once those troublesome spiderlings are still," breathed Spider. Without even looking about him, Spider tucked his eight legs beneath his fat stomach and fell fast asleep within a whisker of Leopard's nose.

In the morning, Leopard awoke first.

"A thousand demons," cried Leopard, astounded to see his strange bedfellow. "Oldman Spider has come to call!"

Then Leopard spied the skeleton of the fish. It was as plain to him as the sleeping spider at his feet just who had been stealing his breakfast from his basket.

"I'll make bones of you, too!" muttered Leopard. "But first I'll teach you a lesson."

Taking the cord from the tail of the fish, Leopard tied it tightly about Spider. When Spider awakened, he was snared as snugly as one of his own catches.

"What is this?" demanded Oldman Spider. Then he caught sight of Leopard's round black eye staring into his own. "Why, why, good morning, dear friend," Spider stammered. "I—I thought to do you a kindness and bring you a fine fat fish. But these are terrible times, and, as I came along, I was set upon by a band of robbers . . ."

Leopard snorted. "Scoundrel!" he growled. "Thief! Trickster! Rascal! Robber! Coward! Liar!" Each time he called out a name, Leopard cracked his huge paw down on Spider's back.

"Mercy!" begged Spider, squirming and struggling. "I'll behave! For evermore!"

"Never!" roared Leopard. "You may fool others, but you don't fool me!"

Had not some of Leopard's blows broken the strands that bound Spider, he would have continued until Spider was little more than a spot on the floor. With one great gasp, Spider tore free. Although his legs were bent beneath him, he managed to stumble from Leopard's den and down the path to home. A cord of his own spinning was still wrapped round his waist.

"Undo me!" cried Oldman Spider when he reached the doorhole of his hut. His wife grabbed hold of the threads tangled around him and pulled. But with each tug the knot grew tighter, until Spider's fat stomach was nearly divided in two.

"I'll snip the cord," suggested Spider's wife, and picked up her yam-cutting knife.

"*No!*" Spider broke out in bumps like a toad. "You'll finish the job by making two halves of my whole!"

There was nothing to do but wait until the twisted threads rotted away from Spider's stomach. That took months, and in all that time he could not swallow so much as a morsel. Spider shrank, smaller and smaller, and his body, pinched in at the waist, looked like an hourglass.

Spider did not act the same, either. He no longer went about boldly by day, for fear of coming face to face with Leopard. Instead, he crept silently in the dark of night and in the dim light of dawn. And all the spider tribe has looked the same and done the same, from that time to this.

As for Firefly, although he shines bright enough for other creatures, he takes care never to come too close to a spiderweb. For who knows what might happen if one meets a tricky fellow like Oldman Spider, even today?

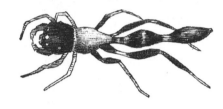

Speaking of Spiders

WHAT does a spider look like, really?

If you answer eight legs, two body parts, and a skinny waist, you're right. But a spider doesn't look the same throughout its life.

A spider wears its skeleton on the outside. When it needs to grow and change, it sheds its old overcoat for a new and larger one. If it accidentally loses a leg, it will replace that, too. Usually spiders keep their original color. But tree tarantulas, who are black with bright pink legs when they're spiderlings, change to pink with black legs when adults. Even without molting, flower spiders can match their hue to the hiding place inside a blossom. There's even one kind of spider who does not look like a spider at all. To fool its enemies, it has disguised itself to look like an ant!

Spiders change to suit storytellers, too. That's why spiders are known by so many different names.

The African peoples brought Ananse with them to the new world. Stories are still told about him in Jamaica, although the spelling is often Anansi or Ananci. But in Haiti, which is French-speaking, the spider tales are about Ti-Jean, or Uncle John. In St. Lucia and Grenada, he's called Compré Czien, Brother Spider.

When Ananse arrived in the United States, there was already a spider-trickster living here. His name was Wihio, which means spider in the Cheyenne tongue. This Indian spider-man was much like his African cousin. In the southern states, Ananse became a lady called Aunt Nancy. If you say it quickly, you'll see how she got her name. In Louisiana, Spider even slipped into a rabbit skin and was magically transformed to Br'er Rabbit!

5

A Web
Around the World

Wise spiders with will weave webs wonderfully well.
                                        —*Tongue twister*

THAT'S more than a tongue twister. It's true.

Because webs get torn or dusty, many spiders make a fresh one every day. Although the web is new, the design is old, for a spider weaves the same pattern again and again. An orb-weaver may use three or four different kinds of silk and connect its spirals at more than a thousand different points, yet it can finish the job of web weaving in half an hour. People everywhere have marveled at the lacy barricade that suddenly stretches, as if by magic, across an opening. And so they told a story.

From different places, and at different times, come similar legends about a spider weaving a web to help out a hero. In Israel, they speak of the spider who helped David escape from Saul. Another version tells of a spider protecting Jesus from Herod. In Italy, it is Saint Feliz who is saved by a spiderweb. And from Japan comes the tale of the web that rescued the warrior Yoritomo.

A legend about Mohammed is repeated worldwide. The name Mohammed means "highly praised," and he became the Prophet of Islam. But at first Mohammed had more enemies than friends, for then people worshipped many household gods and "jinn," while he preached there was only one God, Allah. The leaders of the land feared both the man and his message. "The Prophet and the Spider" tells how a spider saved Mohammed's life.

The Prophet
and the Spider

ALMOST fourteen hundred years ago, in the city of Mecca, in the land of Arabia, there lived a camel driver named Mohammed.

One day a merchant, Abu Bakr, came to Mohammed and pleaded, "Hear me, O Prophet. Even as I speak, there are wicked men who plot to capture and to kill you. You must flee this city at once."

Mohammed knew that what Abu said was true, and he dared not delay for even another hour. Stopping only long enough to fill their goatskin bags with water, the two started north across the barren desert. As a caravan driver, Mohammed was wise in the ways of following the salt trails and camel tracks. But he and his friend had gone only a few miles when a sandstorm suddenly swept about them. The whirlwind flung sand in their faces, stinging their eyes and filling their throats with grit. It blotted out the blazing sun above their heads and erased the path before their feet. With neither bush nor tree for a landmark, Mohammed and his merchant friend were lost.

Then, muffled by the shrieking of the storm, they heard the snorting of horses. That could mean only one thing. Mohammed's enemies had discovered his escape and had come in pursuit.

"Now we are lost indeed," cried Abu Bakr, "for we are but two against many."

"No," replied Mohammed. "We are three, for God is with us."

Mohammed dropped to his knees and asked Allah for help. Almost at once the wind died and the sand sifted back to the ground. When Mohammed lifted his eyes he noticed a large outcropping of rock. Between two huge boulders was a narrow opening.

"See, my friend?" Mohammed pointed. "Allah is watching out for us, for there is our haven."

Abu Bakr looked anxiously behind him, for now a new dust cloud darkened the horizon. This one was raised by the flying feet of the horses.

"There is not time!" he cried. Turning, he saw the rocks and shook his head. "Nor is there room enough. We cannot squeeze through such a crevice."

Mohammed walked calmly to the rock and pushed his forefinger against it. Although the stone weighed many tons, it shifted beneath his touch as if it were no bigger than a pebble. The boulder slid aside until the opening was wide enough for Mohammed to slip within. He beckoned Abu Bakr to follow.

Between the rocks was a small dark cave. When they crept inside the two men had to crouch to keep from hitting their heads. But they were not alone in their shadowy hiding place. The cave was home for a great many eight-legged and six-legged and four-legged and no-legged creatures as well. As soon as Mohammed and Abu crowded in, scorpions and beetles and lizards and snakes scuttled and slithered from the cave. Only a single great spider remained, suspended from a slender strand above Mohammed's head.

"Salaam," said Mohammed, glancing up. "Peace to you."

Abu Bakr shuddered when he saw the spider and swung his goatskin bag at the web.

Mohammed caught his arm. "No," he commanded. " 'To Allah belongs everyone dwelling in the heavens and on earth.' "

"But that spider might sting you!" objected the merchant.

"I fear far more the bite of those who are following us," Mohammed said. "Listen!"

Outside the cave they could clearly hear men's voices. They sat still as the stones surrounding them. Only the spider moved. It swung from its thread on the ceiling and began to weave a netting across the narrow opening

to the cave. Back and forth, up and down, the spider strung its spokes until a mesh completely covered the entrance.

Then they heard someone shout, "Mohammed must be hereabouts! Look, there are fresh tracks in the sand—and this rock has been shifted!"

"You, there, boy!" a different voice ordered. "You are slight enough to crawl in that cave. Take a look!"

"Please, Agha, I cannot!" A shadow fell across the cave's entrance, and a trembling voice added, "A huge and hairy spider is hanging there."

"How could Mohammed be inside, then?" asked another. "He would surely have broken this web and frightened the spider."

"You are right." It was the man who had spoken first. "This web has not been disturbed. Mohammed cannot be concealed in the grotto."

"Then he must be ahead of us," said still another. "Make haste! We are fools to waste time here."

There was the scramble and shouting of men remounting their horses, and once again the sand shook from pounding hooves.

In the cave, all was still. Mohammed looked at the spider, silhouetted against the light that slanted in between the boulders. It sat quietly in the center of its great web like the sun in the sky, surrounded by rays. Mohammed touched his forehead to the floor.

"Thank Allah, Abu Bakr, for thus delivering us from danger."

And the merchant joined the Prophet in prayer beneath the spiderweb.

When they were certain that their enemies had given up pursuit, Mohammed and Abu Bakr continued their journey. This time they did not stray from their path. They even managed to find two camels to carry them and soon reached the safety of the city of Medina.

Because of a spider, the life of the Prophet had been saved. And that is why his followers still spare a spider's life, even today.

Never
Kill a Spider!

FOR some spiders, life lasts for only a season. Others, like trapdoor spiders, may live for twenty-five years. Fortunately for spiders, we have sensible reasons for leaving them alone. We have some not-so-sensible ones as well. These sayings have been around far longer than any spider.

From Britain:

> If you wish to live and thrive,
> Let a spider run alive.

> Kill a spider, bad luck yours will be
> Until of flies you've swatted fifty-three.

In our own country you may hear:

> Do not kill a spider to save your life
> For the spider is the devil's wife.

> Kill a spider, a storm is sure to follow.

> Kill a spider and you'll destroy the new clothes
> it's weaving for you.

> Step on a spider and you will be poor for life.

Should a Teton Indian kill a spider by mistake, he calls out, "Oh, Grandfather Spider, the Thunder-Beings killed you!" Then, he hopes, the spider's spirit will not blame him for its death.

In Tahiti, spiders are believed to be the earthly shadows of the gods and are never harmed in any way.

In Scotland, it was believed that for every spider squashed or swatted, a dish would drop and shatter. Because of the legend of Robert Bruce and the spider, no Scotsman deliberately killed one. But that's another story, and the next to come.

6

Spider's Lifeline

Over in the meadow in a sly little den
Lived an old mother spider and her little spiders ten.
  "Spin," said the mother.
  "We spin," said the ten.
So they spun all day in their sly little den.
from "Over in the Meadow,"
American counting song

ALL spiders spin, but not all of them spin webs. They may use their sturdy thread for ballooning lines, as fishing lines, or for lassoing their prey. Some spin trapdoors to their dens, to wrap their food, or to make nests and nurseries. However it is used, a spider's string is its lifeline.

For their size, the slender strands are stronger than steel wires. They're waterproof and, like rubber bands, can stretch without snapping. Until quite recently, we used delicate spider silk in our telescopes and laboratory instruments and wove some of the thickest into fishing lines and nets. The Chinese used spider silk as sewing thread, and two centuries ago a Frenchman made a pair of gloves and a pair of stockings from spiderwebs.

A single spider has been known to spin one hundred yards of silk in just one hour. Even so, we're not likely to raise spiders for their silk. Spiders need a steady diet of live insects and must be kept apart from one another, or else they'd be too busy snaring their neighbors to tend to their spinning.

In this legend, told throughout Britain, the thread a spider spins serves a purpose for both spider and man. It's called "The Spider and the King."

The Spider
and the King

THE man bent beneath the low frame of the door and peered inside. The hut was scarce big enough to turn about. Lest he took care, he'd whack his helmet on the rafters or scrape his knuckles on the rough stone walls.

"More fit for sheep than shepherd," said the man.

He swung shut the heavy timber door behind him and thrust the crossbar through against the rising wind. "But a safe enough shelter, nonetheless."

Although he spoke only to himself, his voice boomed loud in the little room. There were no windows, and only pale twilight filtered down through the hole in the roof. Beneath the opening was a circle of stones, and in it were piled small chunks of peat.

"Aye!" The man rubbed his hands. "Where there's fuel, a fire will follow. And where there's a smoke hole, smoke's bound to rise."

He crossed the dirt floor and swung his poke down from his shoulder. He pulled a flint from the sack, struck a spark, and blew gently until the peat began to glow. Then he sat down, pulled off his boots, and stretched his feet to the embers.

"Not warmth enough to dry my leggings, much less warm my bones," he grumbled.

A gust of wind whistled down the hole. The fire flickered in the draft, and smoke filled the hut. The man sneezed, unfastened his plaid, and waved it about to clear the air. The cape snagged on a splintered rafter and ripped. As he reached up to loosen it, he saw he'd torn something far more frail. A little gray spider ran across her torn web.

"Och!" the man exclaimed. "A little wild deer! Did not Saint Patrick drive all of ye from Ireland's shores?"

The spider scuttled into a shadowy corner.

"I'll not be chasing ye off," he added. "A shepherd's hut is no castle, but 'tis better than a dungeon, and surely big enough for two."

The spider crept from her cranny.

"I come alone, for my soldiers are scattered the length of Scotland." He sat down again and took off his helmet, running his finger over the circlet of gold about its crown. "Truth to tell, I am a king who's lost both kin and country."

Overhead, the small spider began to repair her web. She struggled to string a bridge from one rafter to another. But her thread fell short of the intended beam.

The man shrugged. "Like ye, I set my sights too high."

The spider threw her silk again, and missed.

"We battled brave enough, but 'twas like throwing Little Folk against the giants." The man shivered and tugged his cape around his shoulders. "The English had horsemen in chain mail and archers with longbows. We Scots had no legs beneath us save our own, and naught but pikes and spears over our shoulders."

The spider stopped her task, as if listening.

"Ye are a canny creature," said the man, "but ye can no understand, for all that. Would I had a beast of a different sort to comfort me this night."

For a third time, the spider spun a strand.

"A hound. My own dog that tagged at my boots since he was yet so young he wobbled when he walked. I raised him to the finest in any hunt. He never tired, nor lost the trail, and 'twas fast as any faery hound."

The man glanced up. Again the spider's thread had slipped.

"But your company is healthier for me. The dog was caught by Englishers, and now 'tis myself he tracks. Each time he whiffs my scent, he howls, that eager to be with me. Once he came so close his breath fair tickled my heels. Had I not waded across a burn, 'tis I who'd be leashed to an English master."

The man bent and blew on the fire. Then he rummaged about in his sack and pulled out an oatcake.

"Would ye share a king's supper?" he called to the spider. In answer, she cast again, and missed.

"Ye'd rather spread a net for other fare." The man nodded. "A stale bannock's not to my taste, either. Yet I eat no worse than any other Scot this night. For we've scorched the fields and burned our stores. Little's left for greedy English hands and empty English stomachs."

The spider spun her thread. This time it caught fast between the two rafters. But as she started across, one end broke free and the spider dangled in midair.

The man clenched his fist. "So they'd hang me from a rope! Edward has put a royal price upon my head, alive or dead." He loosened his fingers. He'd crushed the oatcake. "Do ye blame me for hiding to save my own neck if I can no save Scotland's?"

The spider had clambered up again and was attempting to attach the mainstring. For the sixth time, she failed.

"Don't ye know when ye're beaten?" cried the man, leaping to his feet and scattering the crumbs of the oatcake. "Again and again ye spin, over and over ye throw, and it all counts for nothing at all!"

At his sudden movement, the spider scurried into the shadows.

"Aye. Retreat." The man shook his head. "For if an army of stout men can flee, so may a spider."

As if taking the challenge, the spider ran out again from the corner. She balanced on the edge of the beam, ready to spin once more.

The man caught his breath. Six times he had fought the rule of the English king, and six times he'd been the loser. "Cast again, good neighbor," he said softly. "Though ye do not speak, perhaps ye'll yet give me an answer. Should ye now succeed and place thy string, I vow that I, too, will try once more. Had ye but hands, we'd wet thumbs on it."

The spider spun. The floss sailed out. It wavered, and then, almost as if it had a will of its own, it wrapped around the wood. The spider ran across it, securing the thread from one rafter to the other.

"Well won!" shouted the man. "So I, too, must stand and deliver."

The spider paid him no heed, for with the main-string in place, she'd begun to weave the spokes.

The man spread his plaid beside the dying coals, but not to sleep, for his mind was filled with dreams of another kind. At daybreak, he stood and stretched his cramped legs. At eye level hung the fresh-made spiderweb and, within, the spider.

"My humble thanks," he said. "Though small, thy spirit is great. Now my determination must match thine." He put on his helmet with the circlet of gold, and bowed to the spider.

The man returned to Scotland, gathered a loyal band of men, and in the Battle of Bannockburn drove off the English attackers. As with the spider, on his seventh try he succeeded. Robert Bruce became king of a free and united country.

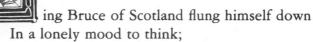

King Bruce of Scotland flung himself down
   In a lonely mood to think;
'Tis true he was monarch, and wore a crown,
   But his heart was beginning to sink.

Now, just at that moment, a spider dropped,
   With its silken filmy clue;
And the King, in the midst of his thinking, stopped
   To see what the spider would do.

It soon began to cling and crawl
   Straight up, with strong endeavor;
But down it came with a slippery sprawl,
   As near to the ground as ever.

Again it fell and swung below,
   But again it quickly mounted;
Till up and down, now fast, now slow,
   Nine brave attempts were counted.

"Bravo, bravo!" the King cried out;
   "All honor to those who try;
The spider up there defied despair;
   He conquered, and why shouldn't I?"

And Bruce of Scotland braced his mind
   And gossips tell the tale,
That he tried once more as he tried before,
   And that time did not fail.

from "King Bruce and the Spider"
by Eliza Cook

7

Spider's
Friends and Foes

Why did the fly fly?
Because the spider spied her.

SCIENTISTS say it is likely that, millions of years ago,
insects first developed wings to get away from spiders.
But it is a good thing for us that a great many of them
don't escape too easily.

Spiders eat more pests than birds, and they do
the job more safely than pesticides. Without spiders, the
earth would be a pretty unpleasant place. We would
be up to our knees in bugs and our stomachs would be
empty, for insects would devour most of the food.

In England and Wales, it is estimated that spiders
catch at least two hundred trillion insects every year.
That's 200,000,000,000,000. If you could put those bugs
in a bag and place them on one side of a giant scale and
then squeeze all the human beings in England onto the
other, the insects that spiders caught would outweigh
the people.

Although spiders are their own worst enemies (for spiders prey on one another), they are among our best friends. That is the fact behind this folktale from Russia, "Father Spider Comes to Dinner."

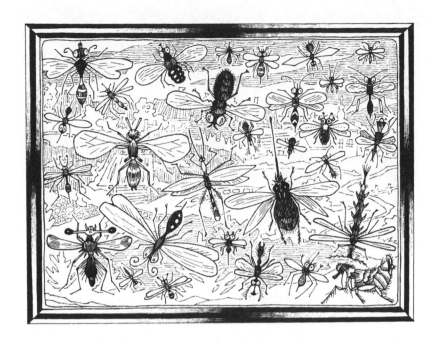

Father Spider
Comes to Dinner

SUMMERS on the steppes of Russia are usually dry. But one year, in the time of the Tsars, rain fell in June, throughout July, and again in August. The dogs and cats—especially the cats—hated the daily drizzles. But the horses and cows were happy, for the grass grew high and they could graze to their stomachs' content. The old men and women complained about the dampness, but the frogs and the children—especially the children— were delighted, for there were dozens of mud puddles to jump over and in.

The mosquitoes and the gnats, the midges and the mites, the flies and the fleas, liked this summer best of all. The wetter the weather, the better for them. Like the grass, they kept growing, both in size and numbers.

After a while the animals, and the people, whatever their ages, were miserable. Everyone itched and scratched. At night, the humming of the mosquitoes was louder than thunder in their ears. By day, flies the size of turnips tracked mud on the ceilings and knocked saucepans from stove tops. Fleas were as big as bumblebees.

One village was so plagued that on an August morning, when the clock in the square struck nine, the town magistrate called everyone together. "Nothing's to be done about the weather," said he, "but something must be done about these buzzing, biting pests."

The villagers were too busy swatting and slapping to answer. Most dared not open their mouths for fear of swallowing a fly. Then one woman, so old and shriveled that even insects found her too dry for their tastes, spoke up.

"When I was a girl, my great-granny talked of a strange animal called Father Spider who lives in the forest beyond the steppes. She said none could match him at gnat catching."

"Ah!" cried the magistrate. "Then we will invite this spider to come and catch as many of the creepers, the crawlers, the biters, and the buzzers as he pleases." He looked around the square. "Who will go into the forest to find Father Spider?"

In the center of the square by the well, a lad named Ivan raised his hand to swat at the mosquito that circled round his head.

"Splendid!" The magistrate smiled. "Brave Ivan has volunteered!"

At once, Ivan was bundled from head to toe in woolen wrappings to protect him from the insects. His mother kissed the tip of his nose, which was all that showed, and rubbed it with pitch from a pine tree so that no bug would be tempted to nip it.

"Now be off," ordered the magistrate, but not unkindly.

"And be home before dark," added his mother.

Ivan had taken only a half dozen steps when he turned back to the square.

"Please," he asked in a voice muffled by the scarf tied over his chin, "how will I know the spider when I meet him?"

No one answered, for none of the villagers had ever seen a spider. Finally the old woman spoke again.

"My great-granny told me that Father Spider could spin." She held up her distaff wound with wool.

Ivan nodded as best he was able and marched down the slippery cobbled street and up the muddy, puddled road. When he reached the woods, he stopped and filled his pockets with pebbles. He scattered them as he went so as to be sure of finding his way home again.

The forest was gloomy, with a musty, mossy smell, and alive with snaps and crackles as creatures scurried away at his approach. Ivan counted fox and marten and deer and skipped a pebble at a hare. He saw the paw prints of bears by his feet, and birds of every feather squawked over his head. But none of these animals could spin, and none looked likely to learn.

As Ivan dropped pebble after pebble, his pockets

got lighter and he walked faster. He could not tell how far he'd come, nor even the time of day, for the tall trees hid the sun. His woolen wraps were hot and scratchy and Ivan's backbone tickled. He was certain a bug or two had been bundled beneath the layers. Then, quite clear and close, he heard the howl of a wolf.

Ivan emptied out his pockets and began to run. One direction was as good as another so long as it was away from the voice of the wolf. As he ran, something stuck to the pitch on the end of his nose. Ivan brushed at it impatiently with a mittened hand.

"Clumsy!" someone scolded. "You've torn my net!"

Dangling above Ivan, almost touching the tassle on his cap, was the queerest animal Ivan had ever laid eyes on. The body was big and brown, but the legs were thin and black, with hairy bristles. Whatever it was began to move in a zigzag pattern, up and down, back and forth, dragging a thread behind it. Although it looked not at all like the little old lady holding her distaff, Ivan was sure it was spinning.

"You're Father Spider!"

"*Tak!*" clicked the creature crossly. "And you are obviously a human thing. Kindly be on your way so I can mend this hole you've made in my web."

"But if it's you," Ivan insisted, "I've come with an invitation."

"I never go out," snapped the spider. "Nor do I let anyone in."

"Please listen, Father Spider," begged Ivan.

The spider, busy tucking and tying his net, paid not the least attention. But Ivan would not give up so easily. He told everything he knew about his village and added a few inventions of his own. The spider yawned. Then Ivan described the mosquitoes, the gnats, the midges, the mites, the flies, and the fleas.

"Such a tempting tale," the spider said. "I seldom accept invitations, for I've my spiderlings to tend to, but you put it so nicely, I cannot refuse."

The spider swung down from his web and began scrambling through the underbrush.

"Wait!" cried Ivan.

"It's rude to be late for supper," called the spider over his shoulder, and was lost to sight.

Ivan feared he was lost too. He did not see one single pebble he had dropped. But, as he searched, he discovered that the thread was still dragging behind Father Spider as he ran. Ivan picked it up and followed, hand over hand, step by step, through the trees, to the road, and all the way back to his village.

Ivan was surprised to find the villagers still in the square. It seemed he'd been gone so long he must have grown at least an inch, but in fact, his whole adventure had taken but one hour and fifty-seven minutes. Everyone was watching this strange thing called a spider. Already it had strung strong lines from the four corners of the square to the well in the middle. By noon, a wonderful web, with one hundred spokes, shimmered in the sunlight. The villagers cheered, and the spider made a small bow.

"I believe it's time to dine," said he.

Ivan, quite hungry after such a walk, went home with the others for a midday meal while Father Spider sat down in the center of his web to await his.

He did not have to wait for long. A gnat, two

moths, and a curious cricket brushed against the netting and were held fast.

"You'd scarcely be a mouthful," sniffed the spider, and continued watching and waiting.

Then a huge fly, intent on making off with a mouse, stumbled into the spiderweb.

"*Tak, tak!*" said the spider, pleased. He tiptoed over to the fly.

"Help!" the fly cried.

"How nice of you to join me!" Father Spider carefully wiped his claws.

"Please," begged the fly, struggling against the sticky ropes, "let me loose. I'll give you anything at all."

"You've already given me plenty." The spider patted his stomach.

"But," said the fly, "I've children at home. Dozens and dozens of them."

"So have I," the spider said, remembering all the small spiderlings left behind in the forest.

"And," cried the fly, "left alone, those little fellows will pester the dogs and the cats."

Spider tied a leaf around his waist for a napkin.

"The dogs will growl and the cats will yowl and all the villagers will blame you. They'll chase you away with their sticks."

The spider thought. Perhaps, at this very moment, his spiderlings were misbehaving, too. He sighed. "Very well. I'll let you go, providing, of course, that you return as soon as your children are cared for."

"Of course! Of course!" cried the fly. "Oh, thank you, Father Spider!"

The spider loosened the knots, and the fly shook its wings and broke free.

"Ho! Ho! Ho!" the fly jeered, hovering high above the web. "Your stupidity is even greater than your appetite! You'll not see me—nor any others—ever again."

And the fly flew off, shrieking, "Stay away from the spider, brothers! He's set a snare to trap you!"

All the mosquitoes and the gnats, the midges and the mites, heard the fly's alarm and hid inside the houses. When the sun went down, the insects came out of their hiding places. In every home they hopped and skittered, fluttered and flitted, nipped and stung. It was worse than before. The menfolk armed themselves with pitchforks and the housewives batted with their brooms. The children pulled the covers over their heads.

"Do something!" shouted the magistrate. None but Father Spider heard him over the buzzing of the bugs.

The spider sat, sad, in his web. He was hungry, for he had long since disposed of the gnat and the two moths. Only the cricket remained. The spider was just about to make a snack of it when a thought struck him with such force that his whole web shook.

"It's possible," said Father Spider, crisscrossing over to the cricket, "to dispatch you in a different fashion!"

The cricket quivered within its bonds.

"You shall go free, friend, and be my messenger."

The cricket chirruped hopefully.

"Play your fiddle and beat the drum," ordered the spider, "and shout the news, 'Spider is dead! Spider is dead! He was called to Kazan and they chopped off his head!'"

"But you aren't dead," objected the cricket.

"No," the spider whispered, "but *you* may be if you don't do as I tell you."

"A bargain!" squeaked the cricket and began hopping around to all the houses and shouting through the shuttered windows, "Spider is dead! Spider is dead!"

Cricket ran up and down the road, playing his fiddle and beating a drum. "He was called to Kazan and they chopped off his head!"

When the other insects heard the cricket's call, they rushed out into the square. The spiderweb was empty.

"We've won! We've won!" sang the fly, and the mosquitoes hummed in chorus, "Father Spider is gone and done!"

The cockroaches waltzed around with the spotted beetles. The mites chased the midges in circles, and the fleas jumped jigs in the square. They all got so giddy that one by one the insects bumped and bumbled into the sticky net. When morning came, every single kind of bug (with the exception of the cricket, who knew better) was hung like a decoration in the spider's web. In the middle sat the spider himself.

"Long live Father Spider!" cried the magistrate and the villagers.

The spider bowed politely once again. But he was much too modest to take all the credit. "It was Ivan who so kindly invited me to dine." The spider smiled as he counted up the company in his web. "Thank you, my friends. No one is more pleased than I with my visit."

Ever after, whatever the weather, the people who live on the steppes have not been so troubled by mosquitoes and gnats or any of their kin. For they make sure to invite Father Spider in to dine. He weaves a web in their rafters and rids them of other, not-so-welcome, guests, while down below, beside the stove, the cricket still fiddles and sings, *"Kazan! Kazan!"*

"Will you walk into my parlor?" said the Spider
to the Fly,
" 'Tis the prettiest little parlor that ever you did
spy;
The way into my parlor is up a winding stair,
And I have many curious things to show when
you are there."
"Oh no, no," said the little Fly, "to ask me is in
vain;
For who goes up your winding stair can ne'er
come down again."

"I'm sure you must be weary, dear, with soaring
up so high;
Will you rest upon my little bed?" said the Spider to the Fly.
"There are pretty curtains drawn around, the
sheets are fine and thin;
And if you like to rest awhile, I'll snugly tuck
you in."
"Oh no, no," said the little Fly, "for I've often
heard it said
They never, never wake again, who sleep upon
your bed!"

Said the cunning Spider to the Fly, "Dear friend, what can I do?
To prove the warm affection I've always felt for you?
I have within my pantry a good store of all that's nice,
I'm sure you're very welcome—will you please to take a slice?"
"Oh no, no," said the little Fly, "kind sir, that cannot be,
I've heard what's in your pantry, and I do not wish to see."

from "The Spider and the Fly"
by Mary Howitt

8

Magic, Make-believe, and Medicine

If a spider falls into the fire,
a witch is waiting nearby.

THAT is a saying from the last century. Before they chose the company of cats, it was thought that witches used spiders as their helpers, or "familiars." As well as casting cobwebby spells, witches might change themselves into spiders.

Long before any witch was around to make mischief, spiders were tied to black magic. Many ancient peoples feared them, and Egyptians prayed to their god Bes for protection from them. Two thousand years ago, Romans carried a special stone—an agate—to ward away spider spells.

Many of the superstitions about spiders began because, until recently, they were considered very dangerous. The old English word for spider was *attercop*, which means "poisonhead." Our word "cobweb" came

89

from this. In 1576, an English author wrote, "Spiders convert to poison whatsoever they touch." But, in fact, only a few spider bites are serious, and only a very few spiders, like the brown recluse or the black widow, can be called dangerous. These shy spiders try to hide and don't bite unless bothered.

Among the scariest of spiders is the tarantula. Four centuries ago, townspeople in the Italian village of Taranto believed that fast and wild dancing was the best cure for its bite. So both the spider and the dance—the tarantella—were named for this town. Another antidote was a lot less fun. If someone was bitten by a *tarentula*, he was rushed to the baker's oven and toasted until he protested. Although it may win the prize for ugliness, the hairy tarantula is quite gentle and makes an interesting pet.

Even today, knowing as much about spiders as we do, some people still shiver at the thought of them. Perhaps that's because spiders silently weave their webs while we are sleeping, or because they dart so quickly when discovered. The long bent legs of the spider make it look threatening and much bigger than it really is. Even the bravest of us sometimes jump when we see a spider.

So we shouldn't blame Marco for fearing spiders in this old fairytale from Portugal, "The Spellbound Spider."

The Spellbound Spider

ONCE upon an early time in Portugal, there lived a shoemaker, his wife, and their son, Marco. The old folks were sensible sorts, but young Marco was a dreamer. He was always make-believing this and pretending that.

"Perhaps a spider spun a spell over Marco," said his mother as she brushed a spiderweb from the ceiling.

A spider! Marco's eyes were shut, daydreaming as usual, but his cars were open.

"The lad's head is stuffed with cobwebs, sure enough," agreed his father.

Marco, peeping from beneath his lids, thought he saw a cobweb stretched between his lashes.

From that moment on, Marco hated spiders. He dreaded reaching into cobwebby cupboards. A bit of thread hanging from his sleeve was enough to make him panic, and he stamped on any spider, real or fancied, that he saw. Even when he napped, spiders crept into his sleep.

"Too much imagination!" said his mother, shaking her head.

"Marco should learn shoemaking," his father decided. "A trade will keep his mind from mischief."

Marco learned to be a cobbler, but not a very good one. Thinking of other things, he would cut out two right shoes, or two left ones. Gazing out the window, he would snip a pattern crooked as a corkscrew, or nail the heel of a boot to the bench. And since the window glass was splintered in the corner like a spiderweb, it sometimes made him start and poke himself with the needle.

His father, weary of undoing and repairing Marco's mistakes, declared, "I cannot do a thing with the boy!"

"Then I will go off to seek my fortune," said Marco cheerfully.

"But," his mother protested, "I had hoped you would settle down and take a wife. . . ."

Marco shrugged. "If that's what will please you, I will ask the first *senhorita* that I meet to marry me."

As usual, Marco spoke without thinking. But what is said is said. Marco took the shoemaking tools and a few pieces of leather that his father gave him and the loaf of fresh bread that his mother baked and stuffed them all in a sack. Then he kissed his mother on the cheek, shook his father's hand, and set out to see the world.

At first, he whistled as he went. But, as he traveled farther, the path got steep and stony, and his feet began to hurt. He had made one boot too big and the other much too small. At last he came to a large cork tree that spread its branches over a flat white stone beside a small stream. Marco sat on the rock and dipped his blistered heel and pinched toes into the cool water. He dug the loaf from his sack but had scarcely bitten into it when he had the strange feeling that someone was spying on him.

"Who's there?" cried Marco, looking about.

He heard only the gurgle of the water. Then he took another bite, and saw, from the corner of his right eye, something creep ever so quietly from beneath the rock.

"Aranha!"

Marco choked on the crust. The largest spider he had ever seen was inching across the stone. He wished it were his imagination, but never, not in his worst nightmares, could he have invented such a horrible, ugly, loathsome spider.

As the spider crept closer and closer, Marco's own silly words echoed in his ear: "I will ask the first *senhorita* that I meet to marry me!" Certainly such a harmless little boast did not deserve punishment like this! But Marco could not break his vow, for he'd made a promise to his mother.

"*Senhorita* Spider," Marco whispered, "will you be my—" he swallowed hard and croaked—*"wife?"*

Marco hoped she would run away. Instead, she hopped onto the loaf of bread and crawled into the hole where he had taken a bite.

"So be it," said Marco, standing up on shaking legs. Holding the bread at arm's length, he again trudged along the trail.

Marco's shadow grew longer as the light from the sun got dimmer. He feared that he and his ugly companion were lost, but at last he saw the arms of an old windmill raised against the evening sky. The sails of the windmill were torn, and the door swung open on broken hinges.

"Perhaps it's haunted." Marco trembled and dropped the bread inside the door. "I daresay *you'll* feel right at home here!"

The spider crawled out of the loaf and scuttled up the doorframe. Across the room, as far away from her as he could get, Marco put down his bundle. Too weary to worry, he laid his head on the sack and fell fast asleep.

He dreamed he was a king living in an ivory palace. It was a wonderful dream until he chanced to look beside him and saw that a spider shared the throne. Marco's eyes flew open. It was morning. The splendid palace was but a windmill, and, just an inch above his nose, dangled his fearsome spider-wife-to-be.

"Get away!" cried Marco.

The spider swung back and forth on her silky thread, saying not a word. It was Marco who got away, running out the door, dragging his sack behind him. By daylight, he saw that the windmill stood atop a steep hill and that a village nestled in the valley below. Marco hurried down, and this time met with good luck. The town had no cobbler, and all the villagers had holes in their shoes. Marco set up shop in the marketplace and began to patch their boots and stitch their slippers. At sunset, he climbed back up the hill, but slowly, for a tumbling-down windmill and a spider within were all that awaited him.

As he drew near, he saw that the sails were mended, waving around in the breeze, and that curtains hung in the windows.

"Well!" exclaimed Marco, too amazed to say anything more.

Each day Marco visited the village to repair or replace the shoes of the grateful townfolk. Soon he'd earned enough to buy a sack of flour, a barrel of olive oil, and a little clay stove. Now when he returned to the windmill in the evenings, the good smell of garlic soup and fresh-baked rolls tickled his nose. The spider also wove, and laces and embroideries on the walls of the windmill feasted his eyes.

How the spider managed all this even Marco could not imagine. He said only, "If it's not my lot to have a lovely wife, it's good to choose a busy one." But he crossed his fingers as he spoke, lest the spider be spinning spells as well. He took care never to get too near her.

By and by, some of the villagers began to complain about Marco's shoemaking. Boots pinched and soles fell from shoes. To make amends, Marco gave them some of the spider's handiwork. Her weavings were so beautiful that folks forgave Marco's shortcomings as a shoe-maker and clamored to buy her cloth. In no time Marco collected enough coppers for a horse and rode up and down the hill, harness jingling.

"What a clever fellow I am!" Marco declared.

Silent as ever, the spider watched from her web.

Marco's spider was as quick as she was quiet. The more she wove, the more Marco sold. By autumn, his sack was stuffed with coins, the cupboard filled with food, and half a dozen hens and a fine-feathered rooster pecked and strutted outside the windmill door.

"Ki ki kiri!" crowed the cock, but the spider made no noise at all.

Although Marco still hated spiders in general, he could scarcely object to this one. She did not trouble him by day and almost never crept into his dreams by night. His thoughts took a more practical turn.

"You stay to your spinning," said he. "I'll get a servant girl to do the rest."

Marco thought he heard the spider sigh, but he could not be sure. He hired a servant girl anyway, but she screamed when she laid eyes upon her ugly, eight-legged mistress.

"Afraid of a spider?" asked Marco, as if he had never heard of such a thing. "She is the best you'll ever serve, for she'll not scold or nag you."

That was true enough, and the strange threesome got along quite comfortably throughout the winter and spring. But as midsummer again grew near, Marco knew it was time to visit his parents. His father was certain to be pleased by his good fortune, but his mother would be less than delighted with her future daughter-in-law.

"Come along with me and pretend you are to be my wife," he whispered in the maid's ear.

The maid nodded. Above Marco's head the spiderweb quivered, and he felt a tear trickle down the back of his neck. For a moment he hesitated.

"You don't understand," he shouted then. "You're only an *insect*!"

Marco turned and ran out the door. He saddled the horse, and he and the servant girl galloped away, neither slowing nor stopping until they reached the great cork tree. There Marco rested, holding his head in his hands. In his mind he again saw the spider creep around the rock and again heard his own words, "*Senhorita* Spider, will you be my wife . . . ?" All was still save for the sound of the brook, and then . . .

"*Ki ki kiri!*" called a rooster.

"Listen, Master," said the servant maid. "Is it not strange for a cock to crow at midday?"

"I didn't hear," said Marco.

"See, Master! It is your own rooster chasing us!"

"I did not notice."

"Look now, Master! Your frightful spider is riding on its head!"

"She is not frightful!" Marco jumped to his feet. "It is I who have been foolish and frightened."

Marco ran to meet the bird and its curious rider and did what he once had thought he never could do. He lifted the ugly spider from the rooster's head and held it gently in his hand. "You shall indeed be my own true wife," declared Marco.

At that, the rooster crowed:

> Ki kiri ki
> Ki kiri kioh!
> Here is the king,
> And there is the queen, oh!

There came a loud rumble, louder than a burst of thunder, and Marco quaked in his mismatched boots. The white stone split open, and in its place rose an ivory palace, with towers and turrets. The stream stilled and became a deep reflecting pool.

"It must be my imagination," said Marco.

The spider stirred within his grasp and Marco looked down. Where once had been eight bent legs were now five soft fingers. He was holding the hand of a beautiful woman. Marco dropped it, embarrassed, and would have galloped off on his horse had she not spoken.

"Do you not know me, Marco?" she asked in a voice low and rusty as if she had not used it for an age. "It is I, your own spider."

Marco was too surprised to speak. He could only listen as she told him she was really a princess, changed into a spider centuries before by a dreadful little demon.

"I would be a spider still had you not broken the enchantment by choosing me of your own free will."

This was better than any of Marco's dreams, but the best was yet to come. As the cock had sung, he became king, the princess his queen. The maid became first lady-in-waiting and Marco's parents a fine duke and duchess.

Marco's mother shook her sensible head and exclaimed, "I cannot believe it!"

But that's just as it happened then, and should you visit Portugal now, you will find the cock sitting on top of the castle tower, as a weathervane. You can see the same old windmill, and, if you look closely, you may find a spiderweb stretched between the sails.

Curious Charms
and Cures

SPIDERS can be charming creatures. Just a few hundred years ago, people wore real spiders as charms. Three spiders hung about the neck, in a bag or walnut shell, were thought to bring down a fever. Our American poet Longfellow mentions such a spider necklace in his tale *Evangeline.* In your great-grandmother's day, tiny spiders were sometimes enclosed in glass and used as dress buttons, both for good looks and good luck.

To cure whooping cough, a spider was dangled over the patient's head while this charm was chanted:

> Spider, as you waste away,
> Whooping cough no longer stay.

As the spider scuttled off, it supposedly carried the disease with it.

Nowadays doctors don't bring spiders on house calls. But in the seventeenth century, the doctor might carry a few spiders in his little black bag, for they were frequently prescribed as medicine. Remember Little Miss Muffet?

> There came a big spider,
> And sat down beside her,
> And frightened Miss Muffet away.

Miss Muffet fled from her tuffet because she'd met quite enough spiders already. Her father, Dr. Thomas

Muffet, often recommended swallowing a spider or two to cure an illness. Even though they were coated with bread crumbs or wrapped up in raisins, spiders were not to Patience Muffet's taste!

Perhaps these other old spider remedies, introduced to this country from Europe, are more to your liking:

To cure malaria, or ague, fasten a single spider to your left arm. If that's not successful, swallow the spider itself with a bit of butter!

Prevent gout by letting spiders run freely about the house (also one of Dr. Muffet's prescriptions!).

Cure asthma by swallowing a ball of spiders' webs.

To rid yourself of warts, rub them with spider silk.

Stop cuts from bleeding by wrapping them with spider webs.

9

Spider
Comes A-Courting

WHEN a spider goes courting, he goes with care and courage. A female spider is usually bigger than the male and might take a hopeful husband for a snack instead of a suitor. The shortsighted web-building spider knows by the feel of the web when he has found a female of his own kind. Then he will serenade her by plucking on one of the strings. Male spiders with sharper eyes, such as wolf spiders, may do little courtship dances or hops and jigs to get the right sort of attention from their would-be mates. Some species of spiders even bring their brides silkwrapped flies as wedding presents. The black widow spider gets her name because she's thought to eat her mate after courtship. But that's not necessarily so. If the bridegroom is both lucky and lively, he can escape her cobwebby parlor.

Spiders are lucky in other marriages, too. In Britain, if a couple sees a spider on their wedding day, then there is thought to be wealth, health, and happiness ahead. Hindus in Bengal, a part of India, collect spiders as special wedding guests for the same reason. In Egypt, good-luck spiders are even slipped into a married couple's bed!

In our own country, in some of our southern states, we say: "A spider on a wedding gown blesses a marriage," and "If a spiderweb is stretched across the path before a courting couple, then there's going to be a wedding."

Also from our south comes this story of a matchmaking spider. It's called, "Sally-Maud, Zachary Dee, and the Dream Spinner."

Sally-Maud, Zachary Dee, and the Dream Spinner

IN THE hills of the Ozarks, up the road a piece from Bean Hollow, and just a hop, skip, and a jump from Henson's Ford, there lived a girl named Sally-Maud.

Sally-Maud was a sight to see. She'd dimples in both cheeks, freckles on her turned-up nose, and hair the color of sugar maples gone red after the frost. She was scarcely bigger than a grasshopper, and every bit as lively on her feet. There wasn't man or boy in those parts who didn't hanker to claim her for his wife. 'Cept Zachary Dee.

But Sally-Maud didn't bat her blue eyes at any of them. She'd toss that fiery head and stick up that pert nose and declare, "I'll have him can treat me best." Then she'd add, "And brings along the best treats besides."

Well, that started off a scramble. Men galloped off to town to fetch sweetmeats in tin boxes and scents in glass bottles and calicos and curios and whatever came to mind. 'Cept for Zachary Dee. He just tipped back in hs chair, whittled on a piece of wood, and watched while others came courting Miss Sally-Maud. Soon there were more goods piled up on that lady's porch than there were in the general store.

"My!" said Sally-Maud, pleased as punch. "Fancy that!" But she never would say who *she* fancied.

In most things, Zachary Dee was the match of any man. He was big and he was strong and so quick he could bag a weasel in the chicken house without even waking the hens. But he was poorer than a flea without a dog. His pockets were empty, save for the holes. He'd nothing but the roof over his head, which leaked when it rained, and the shirt on his back, and it was missing half its buttons. Zack knew he'd never stand a chance with Sally-Maud. That's why, when the rest of the lads slicked up to go sweethearting, Zachary stayed home in his tumbledown shack.

One night, as he was carving out a new wood whistle and listening to the tunes played on a fiddle over at Sally-Maud's, he chanced to look up, and there was a big brown and yellow spotted spider dangling from its thread, right above his head.

"Evening to you, Aunty Longlegs," said Zack.

The spider scuttled back up its silk.

"Glad you've come to visit," Zachary said then. "For I've heard that spiders bring good luck, and it's high time I had a turn of fortune."

Cautiously the spider dropped halfway down again.

"No harm in both of us spinning a few daydreams," said Zack.

The spider began to weave a web, and Zachary Dee began to do some wishful thinking about pretty Sally-Maud. And maybe he dozed a bit, for when he opened his eyes again he had a wonderful idea.

"Thank you kindly, Aunty," said Zack to the spider, for he was certain she'd put the notion in his head.

Straightaway he went to his cupboard and rummaged about until he'd found his dead-and-gone Granny's tortoiseshell hairpin. He'd never seen much use for it before—it was no good as a fish hook—but now Zack knew exactly what to do with it. By the sun's first light, he took that fancy hairpin and buried it beneath a spruce-pine, not far from Sally-Maud's house.

Then he made himself a batch of hoecakes, and when it was full morning, he started back, whistling, toward Miss Sally-Maud's. But he wasn't alone. He was toting Aunty Longlegs, dangling from his fingers like a charm on a string.

Sally-Maud was sitting on her porch in a caneback rocker, looking over all her treasures.

"Morning," called Zack, when he had come up close.

"Good morning to you, Zachary Dee," Sally-Maud answered. Then she pouted a bit, for she was miffed that Zack had never come courting. "Don't see you about here often."

"That's a fact," agreed Zack. "But today I'm out walking my dream spinner."

"Who's that?" asked Sally-Maud, for she couldn't make out what he held in his hand.

"My dream spinner," said Zack again. "Aunty Longlegs here, who makes all my dreams come true." And he swung the spider on its threads beneath Sally-Maud's nose.

"Ugh!" screamed Sally-Maud, jumping back. "That's just a plain old creepy-crawler."

"No, ma'am," insisted Zachary. "Why, only last night, as she spun her web, it came to me—clear as if she'd spoke out loud—where to find a genuine tortoise-shell hairpin."

"Where's that?"

"Why, buried beneath that spruce-pine yonder. You can go look for yourself, if you please."

Sally-Maud did please, and quick as could be she was on her hands and knees, scratching about in the dirt beneath the spruce-pine. Soon enough she found the hairpin.

"If that don't beat all!" she exclaimed.

"Keep it, if you want," said Zack. "I don't hold much for hairpins myself, and it goes right well with your red hair."

Then he turned and started back home.

"Wait!" cried Sally-Maud. "Would you maybe be coming to call with the others tonight?"

Zachary Dee shook his head. "No. Aunty Longlegs

here is too busy spinning nighttimes to go calling, and I'd not leave her alone." He put the spider gently on his shoulder and walked back to his cabin. Sally-Maud just stood open mouthed, staring after the both of them.

Zack hung the spider back in its web. She set right to mending it, and he sat down to whittle on his whistle. After a bit he got up and rummaged in his cupboard again. At the back of it he found his grandaddy's old pocket watch. It hadn't ticked off a minute for fifty years, but the chain it hung from was good as new. So Zack snapped off the watch and took the chain and put it beneath a rock, halfway between his cabin and Miss Sally-Maud's.

Next day, he plucked the spider from its web once more. "Time for an airing, Aunty Longlegs," said he, and the two started off, just as they had on the morning before.

"Howdy!" called Sally-Maud, soon as she saw him.

"Howdy yourself," said Zack.

"Are you walking your dream spinner?" she asked, patting the tortoiseshell pin in her hair.

"That I am," said Zachary, "for last night Aunty Longlegs told me where to find a shiny silver chain."

"Where?" Sally-Maud cried, all excited.

"Where?" asked Zachary Dee, swinging Aunty Longlegs around on her slender thread. The spider seemed to point a leg.

"Beneath that big old rock back yonder," said Zack.

He and Miss Sally-Maud walked hand in hand back to the rock. Sure enough, that's where she found the chain.

"Well, I never!" she exclaimed.

"I never, either," agreed Zack. "It's all Aunty Long-legs' doing. But I don't need shiny chains, and Aunty here can spin her own. Keep it, if you like."

Then Zachary Dee fastened the silver chain about Miss Sally's pretty neck.

Sally-Maud smiled and showed her dimples and said, all sweet and soft, "Come up on the porch and set a spell, Zack."

"No, ma'am." He shook his head. "Aunty here is tuckered out." And he put the spider on his shoulder and started home again.

No music came from Sally-Maud's that night, so Zachary reckoned she had sent her suitors home early so's to get a good night's sleep. But Zack himself couldn't catch his forty winks. His brains were in a stew. He'd nary a thought how to woo Miss Sally next, since his cupboard was picked clean of trinkets. As he pondered, he looked up at the spider, and it was as if she spelled out the answer as she spun.

"Thank you kindly, Aunty," said Zack, for now he knew where to find exactly what he needed.

When he went by Sally-Maud's next day, she was standing on the step awaiting him. She looked fresh as a morning glory, and she was wearing both the hairpin and the chain.

"Where's your dream spinner?" asked Sally-Maud, first thing.

"Home and resting. She worked quite a spell last night."

"Did she tell you what to look for?"

"She did indeed," Zack answered. "She bid me get some threepenny nails and fix my roof before it rained."

Sally-Maud looked downright disappointed. Nonetheless, "Whereabouts?" she asked, for she was always ready to go treasure hunting.

"Right here."

"Here?"

"Sure enough. Haven't you got some nails to spare?"

As a matter of fact, just the week before, Henry Biggs the hardware man had brought a whole bucket of brand-new nails to Sally-Maud.

"That old spider! She knows everything!" Sally-Maud giggled and pointed to the nails on the porch.

Zack helped himself to a handful. "This'll do to mend my roof," he said.

"That shirt needs mending, too," said Sally-Maud. "While you're atop your roof, I'll just sew some buttons on it."

So, while Zachary Dee fixed his roof, Miss Sally-Maud fixed his shirt, and washed it, too. He looked mighty smart when he ambled round next morning.

"Have you your dream spinner today?" Sally-Maud called out.

"She's home, tying her web. All that pounding on the roof shook it something terrible."

Sally-Maud sighed.

"Anyway, she told me to fetch some calico curtains for the windows, so's the sun won't get in her eyes while she's working."

"I got some calico," offered Sally-Maud.

"Aunty Longlegs thought you might."

"And I can sew it up into curtains."

"Can you, now? My, that sure will tickle Aunty Longlegs."

All that day Sally-Maud snipped and stitched. That evening Zachary Dee and Aunty Longlegs were snug as could be in their cabin, with the windows shut and the curtains drawn. And if there was any tune played on a fiddle over at Sally-Maud's that night, neither of them heard it.

So it went, each day like the one before, with Zack coming to see Miss Sally-Maud. Sometimes he carried Aunty Longlegs in one hand, sometimes he didn't, but he always went home with something in both hands. Once it was a mirror he said that Aunty'd dreamed about. Another time it was a spider frying pan, for of course she'd fancy that. Soon Sally-Maud's porch was bare of treasures, for most everything that her suitors brought of an evening ended up in Zachary's cabin the following morning. He had hung the looking glass over the chimneypiece, and there was a silk pillow on his chair and two or three tins of cookies in the cupboard.

By and by Sally-Maud said to Zack, "I surely would like to come over and see your place. It must be mighty grand."

"Oh, no!" said Zack. "You can't do that, Sally-Maud."

"Why ever not?" she demanded.

"Because Aunty Longlegs has spun her web right over the doorjamb. None can come in but me—or maybe my bride, if I carry her over the threshold."

"That old dream spinner *told* you that?"

"In a manner of speaking," said Zack. "But I've not yet asked her where I'm to look for a wife."

"Well!" Sally-Maud shook her shiny red locks and stamped her foot so hard she shook the porch. "You might just look right here. And you might ask *me* instead!"

So Zack did, and they were wed, soon as the preacher came by. The three of them, Sally-Maud and Zachary Dee and Aunty Longlegs, lived happily together with everything at hand they'd ever dreamed of.

The Enchanted Web

DID that really happen?

Most of the stories in this book are make-believe. Even those about real people have had imaginary bits and pieces added over the years. But this is a true story.

Once there was a very rich man in Louisiana named Charles Durand. Just before the outbreak of the Civil War, two of his daughters were married in the most splendid wedding ever seen in those parts. Tables were piled high with food. There was music, dancing—and thousands of spiders! A few days before the ceremony, Monsieur Durand imported crates of giant spiders and set them loose in the trees that bordered the drive to his plantation. The canopy of cobwebs that they wove from tree to tree was sprayed with gold dust and shavings of silver. The brides and their grooms drove down a three-mile aisle beneath this roof of sparkling spider lace. Folks still talk of the spectacle, but none can say what became of the eight-legged wedding guests.

Probably you won't invite any spiders to your wedding. But, asked or not, a spider is often our guest. Sooner or later, even now, you will see one spinning in your own garden or hiding in a corner of your closet. After reading this book, you may feel like you've met an old friend. Perhaps, like storytellers of long ago, you will get caught up in its enchanted web and tell a tale yourself.

I hope that's true, too.

But Charlotte's children and grandchildren and great-grandchildren, year after year, lived in the doorway. Each spring there were new little spiders hatching out to take the place of the old. Most of them sailed away, on their balloons. But always two or three stayed and set up housekeeping in the doorway.

from Charlotte's Web
by E. B. White

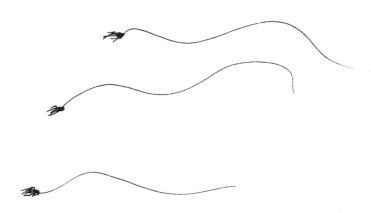

Extras and Explanations

1. SOMEONE SAW A SPIDER

PAGE 3   Remains of early man date from 300,000 years ago, but spider fossils are 300 million years old! A cave painting in Castellón, Spain, shows a spider catching flies.

Estimates of different kinds of spiders range from 30,000 to over 100,000. You may never see the biggest, fifteen inches from leg to leg, for it lives in the jungles of South America. Even if you visit Australia, you will probably not see the smallest, either, for it measures less than 1/35 of an inch.

Arachne's Gift

PAGE 5   Roman names are used for the gods and goddesses in this Greek myth. That's the way that Ovid, a Roman poet, wrote it down, and his story is the source for this particular version. The following key will help you to identify these deities mentioned in the story.

Greek	Roman	
Zeus	Jupiter	king of the gods
Hera	Juno	queen of the gods
Athena	Minerva	goddess of wisdom and the arts, including spinning and weaving
Apollo, later Helios	Apollo	god of the sun
Artemis	Diana	goddess of the moon and hunting
Poseidon	Neptune	god of the sea

PAGE 6   Nymphs were beautiful maidens, divine but not goddesses. They lived in woods, pools and rivers, and on mountaintops.

PAGE 7   The owl was symbol of Minerva's wisdom. Even today, we still consider the owl to be a wise old bird.

PAGE 8   *Minerva*: Since this goddess was also a mighty warrior, she wore battle dress.

PAGE 12   *Aconite*: In the olden days, bitter juices from the roots and leaves of this plant were used to soothe pain.

Arachne no longer needed nose, ears or fingers, for spiders smell, hear, and feel with their legs.

Arachne's Gifts

PAGE 13   *Arachnida* is a class. Within that class spiders belong to an order, *Araneae*. Within that order are fifty-three families of spiders.

2. COBWEBS IN THE SKY

PAGE 15   *Cobwebs*: When we think of spiderwebs, we usually think of the kind that look rather like lacy wagon wheels. But those cobwebs in the corner are spiderwebs, too. Although not so neat as those spun by the orb weavers, they serve their spider owners very well as tents and traps.

The Cloud-Spinner

PAGE 17   *Geta*: Wooden outdoor sandals.

Kimono: A loose robe worn by both men and women. The word *kimono* is both singular and plural.

PAGE 18   *The Hour of the Ox*: The Japanese used to tell time differently than the Western world. The Hour of the Ox is about 1:00 A.M.

PAGE 20   *Goblin-spiders*: Of the many Japanese stories about goblins, some of the scariest were about spiders. Goblin-spiders lurked in dark pools or hid within temples at night.

Spiders turn their food into liquid and sip it. They could not possibly swallow cotton. Their thread is spun from "spinnerets," glands in their abdomens.

PAGE 21   *Kyoto*: The ancient capital of Japan.

PAGE 22   Should a snake wish to, it could doubtless catch a spider. But spiders can scuttle very fast. In England, they used to hold spider races and place wagers on the winner.

3. SPIDERS, SUN, AND SHOWERS

PAGE 27   Many cultures connected the spider to the heavens. In African lore, the sun maidens came down to earth on cobwebs to get water. The Tahitians tell a myth about a spider creating heaven and earth from a huge clam shell, making the sky from the top half of the shell and land from the bottom.

The Spider Brothers Make the Rainbow

PAGE 29   The Achomawi Indians lived along the Pit River in northern California.

PAGE 30   The coyote was often a magical creature in Indian lore. Some tribes even credited him with creating the world.

Sixty sons: Since most spiders lay about one hundred eggs at a time, sixty spiderlings is no great number. Although most adult spiders live alone, sometimes smaller spiders share a web for protection and provision.

Old-Man-Above: A sky-dwelling god, similar to the Great Spirit of some other Indian tribes.

PAGE 31   *Mount Shasta*: This snow-covered peak is more than two and a half miles high, so a trek to the top is a very hard climb.

PAGE 36   *Think*: The Achomawi believed in thought creation. Just by concentrating on an idea, it might actually happen.

Spider the Weatherman

PAGE 40   *Tarantulas*: All spiders need water to live. But for those whose homes are burrows in the ground, a downpour means mud slides and washouts. So tarantulas in California migrate to high ground in the fall before the winter rains begin. The Chicchansee saying is as true today as it was five hundred years ago.

4. SPIDER, THE STORY SPINNER

PAGE 41   Another proverb that suits this story is: "Woe to him who trusts Ananse!"

Ananse means spider in the Twi tongue, which is the chief language of West Africa. Since he owns all the tales and stories told, they are called *Ananse-sem*. The Akan people sometimes called him Kwaku Anansi, or Uncle Anansi, while the Hausa named this trickster-hero Gizo.

How Spider Got His Waistline

PAGE 44   The leopard was an animal both feared and respected and appears almost as often as the spider in African tales.

Wolf spiders and other primitive spiders live in dens or burrows in the ground. They hunt for their food rather than trying to trap their prey in webs.

PAGE 45   Spider needed Firefly's light, for, although most spiders have eight eyes, some are shortsighted.

PAGE 47   A few water spiders actually do catch small fish.

Speaking of Spiders

PAGE 53   All spiders' bodies are divided into two main parts: a combination head and thorax joined by a narrow waist to an abdomen.

Flower spider: This crab spider can change from yellow to white or pink to match the blossom. But spiders may be found in every color of the rainbow—even red or blue—as well as in gray and black and brown like the small ones we see around our homes.

5. A WEB AROUND THE WORLD

PAGE 55   Although spiders may spin new webs daily, they can "recycle" the old web by swallowing and absorbing the silken threads. Spiders who weave longer-lasting orbs sometimes weave thick bands across the center as "keep off the web" signs to butterflies or birds who might rip the net.

PAGE 56   *Jinn*: Spirits able to take either animal or human form. The word "genie"—the kind that popped out of Aladdin's lamp—comes from this root.

The Prophet and the Spider

PAGE 57   Mohammed's name is also spelled Mohomed or Mahomet.

Mohammed was pursued by a religious group called the Coreishites.

PAGE 59   In some versions of this legend, a pigeon is also in the cave. She continues to sit quietly on her nest and so helps to convince Mohammed's enemies that no one is inside.

PAGE 61   *Agha*: A title of respect like "sir."

PAGE 62   After Mohammed's death, Abu Bakr became his successor, or caliph.

6. SPIDER'S LIFELINE

PAGE 65   Since all spiders spin, our name for them fits well. "Spider" comes from the old English *spinnan*, which means "to spin."

The Spider and the King

PAGE 67   Some people believe the setting for this story is Ireland. Others claim it took place in France, or on the Scottish island of Arran. Whether Robert Bruce found shelter in a hut or in a cave is also in question. There are even those who say it never happened at all. But it's a good tale, nonetheless.

PAGE 68   *Plaid*: A cloak worn in the Scottish highlands that fastened over one shoulder and was woven in tartan design.

Saint Patrick: For centuries it was believed that Saint Patrick drove spiders as well as snakes from Ireland and that neither creature dared step or slither over any Irish soil.

Little wild deer: The Gaelic name for spider is *mamhan*

allaidh. It means a little wild deer, perhaps because spiders, like deer, run so swiftly when frightened.

PAGE 69   *Faery hound:* The faery hounds of Scottish stories outrace the wind itself and are green from nose to tail.

Burn: A stream or creek.

PAGE 71   *Edward:* Edward II, king of England.

PAGE 72   *"good neighbor":* An old and friendly term for one of the Little People, or faeries (fairies).

"Wet thumbs on it": A practice much like shaking hands to seal a bargain. Each man licked his thumb and pressed it against his partner's.

Battle of Bannockburn: A fierce combat between English and Scottish forces fought in 1314. Scotland won independence and Robert Bruce secured his right to the throne.

Robert Bruce: The first king of Scotland's name was actually Robert de Brus. His ancestors came from Normandy, and Brus was their home in France. Gradually that became Robert the Bruce, and now it is usually written simply as Robert Bruce.

King Bruce and the Spider

PAGE 73   Although English poet Eliza Cook mistakenly credits the persistent spider with nine attempts instead of seven, children on both sides of the Atlantic have loved this verse for over a century.

7. SPIDER'S FRIENDS AND FOES

PAGE 75   Because spiders are such good pest controllers, they are occasionally air-dropped into an area where there is a bad bug infestation. Even spiders we sometimes fear are more friends than foes. Black widows, for instance, eat the Japanese beetles that often plague our gardens. In Indonesia, it's bad luck to kill any spider because it helps to control cockroaches.

Father Spider Comes to Dinner

PAGE 77   *Steppes*: A steppe is the Russian name for heath or open land. The steppes are vast treeless plains.

Tsar: Emperor, sometimes spelled "czar."

PAGE 79   *Distaff*: The stick that holds the wool or flax in hand spinning.

PAGE 80   *Hairy bristles*: All spiders wear hairy overcoats, although often the bristles are not visible to the human eye. The hairs on a tarantula protect it from harm, for touching them can cause itching and even makes a nosy coyote sneeze!

"Tak!": "So!"

PAGE 81   *One hundred spokes*: Father Spider spun a super web, for a typical orb weaver makes a web with only thirty-nine spokes, or radii.

PAGE 83   *Claw*: A spider's legs end in tiny claws.

PAGE 84   *Kazan*: A city in Russia near the Volga River.

The Spider and the Fly

PAGE 87   This is only half of Mary Howitt's famous poem. An American, she lived from 1799 until 1888.

8. MAGIC, MAKE-BELIEVE, AND MEDICINE

PAGE 90   A spider has no teeth, so even though its jaws are strong for its size, its bite is usually not harmful— unless you're a beetle. Although the black widow's venom is fifteen times more potent than a rattlesnake's, its tiny glands have only 0.060 milligrams of poison. That's still enough to be quite serious, and to warn us to leave them alone, but your chances of ever dying from a spider bite are far less than being struck by a bolt of lightning.

The Spellbound Spider

PAGE 92 *Senhorita*: An unmarried woman; a Miss.

PAGE 93 *Aranha!*: The Portuguese word for spider. Since this noun ends in *a,* a feminine ending, Marco assumes the spider is female.

PAGE 94 Portuguese windmills are sometimes fifty feet tall, with giant blades or sails. Windmills were used for pumping water, and many still stand today.

PAGE 97 The symbol of Portugal is the rooster, the Barcelos Cock, a brightly colored bird whose crow proclaims the triumph of good over evil. It often appears in old Portuguese tales.

PAGE 98 Spiders aren't insects, but Marco certainly wasn't the first to make that mistake. It's only recently that scientists have classified them as arachnids.

Curious Charms and Cures

PAGE 102 Don't laugh too soon at these old-fashioned doctors and their doses. For, a century ago, scientists discovered *arachnidin*, a fever-reducing drug made from—you guessed it—spiderwebs!

9. SPIDER COMES A-COURTING

Sally-Maud, Zachary Dee, and the Dream Spinner

PAGE 107 *Ozarks*: Hilly uplands in Missouri and Arkansas.

PAGE 108 *Aunty Longlegs*: A combination of Daddy Longlegs and Aunt Nancy, the nickname for a spider in the South.

PAGE 115　*Spider frying pan*: A skillet with legs to use over an open fire.

PAGE 116　*Happily ever after*: There's a saying in the Ozarks that if a spider spins a web with your initials in it near a door, then you'll be lucky forever. Surely a spider clever as Aunty Longlegs had no trouble at all weaving an *S* and a *Z* in her web.

The Enchanted Web

PAGE 118　Should you really become a "spider person," then you are on your way to becoming an *arachnologist*—someone who studies spiders.

Bibliography

With special acknowledgment to W. S. Bristowe, author of *The World of Spiders* (London: Collins, 1971), whose interest in spiders from leg to legend inspired my own.

SPIDER FACTS

Lavine, Sigmund A. *Wonders of the Spider World.* New York: Dodd, Mead and Co., 1966.

National Geographic. "What's So Special About Spiders," pp. 190–219. Washington: National Geographic Society; August, 1971.

Naylor, Penelope. *The Spider World.* New York: Franklin Watts, 1973.

Patent, Dorothy Hinshaw. *The Lives of Spiders.* New York: Holiday House, 1980.

————. *Spider Magic.* New York: Holiday House, 1982.

Rood, Ronald. *Animals Nobody Loves.* New York: Bantam Pathfinder Books, 1972.

Shuttlesworth, Dorothy E. *The Story of Spiders.* New York: Doubleday and Co., 1959.

Victor, Joan Berg. *Tarantulas.* New York: Dodd, Mead and Co., 1979.

von Frisch, Karl. *Ten Little Housemates.* London: Pergamon Press, 1960.

Walther, Tom. *A Spider Might.* San Francisco: Sierra Club Books. New York: Charles Scribners' Sons, 1978.

World Book Encyclopedia. Chicago: World Book–Childcraft International, Inc. 1980.

SPIDER FICTION

Appiah, Peggy. *Tales from an Ashanti Village*. New York: Pantheon Books, 1966.

Arkhart, Joyce Cooper. *The Adventures of Spider*. Boston: Little, Brown and Co., 1964.

Bulfinch, Thomas. *Bulfinch's Mythology*. Edited by Elenore Blaisdell. New York: Thomas Y. Crowell Co., 1976.

Coolidge, Olivia. *Greek Myths*. Boston: Houghton Mifflin Co., 1949.

Creel, J. Luke. *Folktales of Liberia*. Minneapolis: T. S. Denison and Co., 1960.

de Leeuw, Adele. *Indonesian Legends and Folktales*. New York: Thomas Nelson and Sons, 1961.

Fisher, Anne B. *Stories California Indians Told*. Berkeley: Parnassus Press, 1957.

Huber, Miriam Blanton, ed. *Story and Verse for Children*. New York: MacMillan Co., 1940.

Lee, F. H., ed. *Folk Tales of All the Nations*. New York: Tudor Publishing Company, 1946.

Robbins, Ruth. *How the First Rainbow Was Made*. Oakland: Parnassus Press; Boston: Houghton Mifflin Co., 1980.

Sakade, Florence, ed. *Japanese Children's Favorite Stories*. Rutland, Vermont; Tokyo, Japan: Charles E. Tuttle, 1958.

Sherlock, Phillip M. *Anansi the Spider Man*. New York: Thomas Y. Crowell and Co., 1954.

Tolstoi, Alexei. *Russian Tales for Children*. New York: E. P. Dutton, 1947.

The World Book Encyclopedia, vols. 1, 2, and 15. Chicago: The Quarrie Corporation, 1939.

SPIDER FOLK BELIEFS

Botkin, B. A., ed. *A Treasury of Southern Folklore*. New York: Bonanza Books, 1980.

Brown, Frank C. *North Carolina Folklore*, vols. 6 and 7. Durham, N.C.: Duke University Press, 1967.

A Dictionary of British Folktales in the English Language. Part B, *Folktales,* vol. 2. Bloomington: Indiana University Press, 1972.

Lee, Albert. *Weather Wisdom.* New York: Doubleday and Co., 1976.

Sarnoff, Jane, and Ruffins, Reynold. *Take Warning! A Book of Superstitions.* New York: Charles Scribners' Sons, 1978.

Schwartz, Alvin. *Cross Your Fingers, Spit in Your Hat.* New York: J. B. Lippincott, 1974.

Schwartz, Alvin. *Flapdoodle.* New York: J. B. Lippincott, 1980.

Sloane, Eric. *Folklore of American Weather.* New York: Duell, Sloan and Pearce, 1963.

Standard Dictionary of Folklore, Mythology and Legend. Edited by Maria Leade. New York: Funk and Wagnalls, 1972.

And with thanks to Dr. Jack A. Friedman and to the Lowie Museum, University of California, Berkeley, for access to their collection of folk beliefs.